Happy Flower Arranging!

With love,

Alan

Christmas 1996

Floral
Crafts

Floral Crafts

Edited by Allen D. Bragdon

Watson-Guptill Publications
New York

Editor: Allen D. Bragdon
Editorial Production: Carolyn Walsh Zellers
Cover Design: John B. Miller, For Art Sake, Inc.

First published in 1994 by Watson-Guptill Publications,
a division of BPI Communications, Inc.,
1515 Broadway, New York, NY 10036

Library of Congress Cataloging-in Publication Data

Floral crafts / edited by Allen D. Bragdon.
      p.   cm.
    ISBN 0-8230-1841-5
    1. Nature craft.   2. Decoration and ornament—
Plant forms.   3. Wreaths.   4. Potpourris
(Scented floral mixtures).   5. Flower arrange-
ment in interior decoration.   I. Bragdon, Allen D.
    TT857.F58   1994
    745.92—dc20   94-7966
                                  CIP

Distributed in the United Kingdom by
Phaidon Press, Ltd., 140 Kensington Church Street,
London W8 4BN, England.

Distributed in Europe (except the United Kingdom),
South and Central America, the Caribbean, the Far
East, the Southeast, and Central Asia by Rotovision
S.A., Route Suisse 9, CH-1295 Mies, Switzerland.

Printed in South Korea

First printing, 1994.

1 2 3 4 5 6 7 8 9

02 01 00 99 98 97 96 95 94

CREDITS & ACKNOWLEDGMENTS

Pages 12, 27: Wreaths and garlands designed by
Jean Howe Goldstein. Photos by John B. Miller

Page 18: *Decorative Doors* photo by Roedel
Photographers.

Pages 34-37: Pressed flower designs by Suzanne
Baybutt, Pressed Floral Graphics, Dennis, MA.

Page 38: Desk set designed by Marjorie Meyer,
Harwich, MA

Page 42: Dried flower arrangements designed by
Wendi Smith, Harvest of Barnstable, MA.

Page 54: Rose beads instructions by Betty Wold,
Gore, OK; necklace by Barbara Tamasi, Dennis,
MA

Page 71: "Mother and Child in a Boat" painting
by Edmund C. Tarbell, poster reproduced with
permission of the Museum of Fine Arts, Boston.

Page 72: Baskets designed by Peach Tree
Designs, Cape Cod, MA. Photo by Ned Manter.

Page 79: Pierced lamp shades courtesy of
Barfield's, Yarmouthport, MA.

Pages 80 & 81: Theorem paintings of bowl of fruit
and tray of fruit courtesy of Education Collection
of the Museum of American Folk Art, New York
City, Gifts of Hirsch & Adler, and of Robert
Bishop.

Page 83: Theorem painting of fruit, bird and but-
terfly courtesy of the collection of the Museum of
American Folk Art, New York City, Gift of Robert
Bishop and Gift of Mrs. William P. Schweitzer.

Page 84: Roses and ribbons needlepoint design
© 1989 by Erica Wilson.

Pages 86, 88-89: Garden design and photo by
Sundial Herb Garden, Higganum, CT.

Pages 94-97: Baskets designed by Cathey Portrie.

Page 99: Wheat weaving design by Barbara
Radcliffe Rogers.

Page 106: Rosebud accents designed by Peg
Famino, Salem, MA.

The projects in this volume have been selected
from *American Pastimes*, an 18-volume work on
traditional folk handcraft techniques and designs
edited by Allen D. Bragdon.

EDITOR'S PREFACE

For the most part this collection of traditional craft designs uses traditional natural materials rather than synthetic copies of nature. Since nature does not do anything exactly the same way twice, these projects invite experimentation. The designs are forgiving for the same reason. You needn't think you failed if *your* finished work does not exactly match the photograph of *our* finished work. Variation is inherent in the materials and experimentation is the path to creative originality. That said, we have taken care, anyway, to supply you with very specific lists of the materials we used and the steps to achieve the same result. When a modern material, such as an adhesive or finish, will do the job as well as the one traditionally used in the past, but with less tedium, we specify it.

Please use this book as you might use a Bible—as a source of inspiration with some useful advice that has worked over time. It does not pretend to be a "bible" that dictates the one true way you must do everything. Use it as a source of ideas to adapt to your own taste in color, your preference for size, the materials that you have available. Perhaps copying exactly is good training in learning how to duplicate an effect. However, the most exciting results of creative effort usually come from some original way of combining elements or a lucky accident—which, not incidentally, accounts for the charming appeal of most folk art.

After all, when most of us cook we often substitute ingredients and vary quantities to suit practical availabilities, our personal taste and to feed our sense of adventure. Similarly, piecework quilters commonly use the same block patterns that have been used for generations to create spectacularly fresh effects, simply by combining available fabrics of varying colors and shades in their own way. As an old Kentucky quilter once put it, "God gives you the pieces, but it's up to you how you put them together."

Now to some housekeeping details:

About Patterns: We hate having to enlarge designs printed small on grids in order to arrive at a workable pattern. That practice is frustrating, often inaccurate and now out of date. For this book we have printed the large patterns full size on foldout sheets that are perforated along their bound-in edge so you can tear them out neatly without damaging the book. Photocopy or trace the smaller patterns printed on the book pages so they will be more convenient to work from.

Iron-on Transfers: On one of the large sheets the patterns are printed with a special heat-transfer ink that melts when the paper is heated by ironing it. These designs are printed in reverse so you can lay them, ink-side down, onto the cardboard, paper, fabric or other flat, smooth material you want to copy them onto. Iron the back of the paper with a dry iron as you would for a delicate fabric (hotter for transferring onto dark-colored material). Although the design will transfer more than once, use it to make one permanent template—of cardboard, for example—for cutting patterns, rather than ironing the pattern onto the fabric each time you use it.

Copying: Almost all copy shops now can copy directly from your book page, and even enlarge or reduce whatever is printed on it to any size you want. We know that a pattern or chart on a separate sheet is much easier to work from and carry in a workbasket than a book is. Therefore, we herewith give you legal permission to make a photocopy of any of our patterns and designs for your own use (not to sell). If you want to make multiple copies for a school class, please write to the publishers (the address is on the facing page) and they will try to work something out.

Hints: ✏ Whenever we know of a shortcut, an alternate way to do something, a caution about a tricky part or some other bit of advice, we have printed it in italic type with that little symbol at the beginning.

Designs and Materials: We selected designs that have been used traditionally and have proven their appeal over the years. Many of these designs have appeared in museum collections, as well as old records and other books. We have reproduced them here, along with the traditional handcraft techniques necessary to recreate them, because they represent traditions worth preserving. We listed the materials and tools needed for each project in the order you will use them when you assemble it.

We placed a color photo or drawing of each finished project on the left-hand page, usually, with the instructions facing it or sometimes continuing on the next page. The title of each project appears next to the page number at the bottom of the right-hand page. The name of the chapter is printed in capital letters next to the page number on the left-hand page.

Our greatest hope is that somewhere in this book you may discover a skill you did not know you possessed and that it will allow your natural creative instincts to grow and flower so you can pass your own delight in them on to others .

— Allen D. Bragdon, Editor

CONTENTS

FROM THE FIELD & GARDEN

Camellia

Sweet Pea

Snapdragon

Azalea

Bells of Ireland

Daffodil

Nasturtium

Hydrangea

Yarrow

Iris

"Rosemary for Remembrance"

Did you know that in Victorian times red camellias proclaimed, "You're a flame in my heart"; yellow lilies boasted, "I'm walking on air"; and spider flowers slyly suggested, "Let's elope"? Just for fun, look at the flowers in the illustration above and guess what they mean. Then turn to our Dictionary of the Language of Flowers beginning on page 10 and see how well you speak this eloquent language. You'll quickly learn that a carefully planned floral message is much more colorful and fragrant and a lot more fun than a thousand written words.

Throughout history, people have given flowers and herbs symbolic meanings from their mythical histories and associations, and out of these meanings grew "languages of flowers." Frescoes and coins found in Bronze Age ruins on Crete and Rhodes depict wild roses that grew abundantly in the area and became a symbol of the locale; ancient Greeks dedicated flowers to the gods and crowned their great citizens with wreaths of blossoms and leaves. In the Roman Empire, rose petals carpeted banquet halls and streets, and anything said "sub rosa" (under the rose) would be held in confidence. In the Middle Ages, flowers became symbols of Christian virtues, associated with religious legends and the Code of Chivalry.

French and English travelers brought the concept of a language of flowers to Europe from Turkey in the mid-18th century. Lady Mary Wortley Montague, wife of an English ambassador to Turkey, wrote to a friend, " . . . you may quarrel, reproach, or send letters of passion, friendship, or civility, or even news without ever inking your fingers." The idea caught on, first in France, then England and America. By the 19th century, "florigraphy," the "science of sweet things," was the subject of many serious "grammar" books and dictionaries, for now arrangement and composition were as significant as the meaning of the flower itself. For instance, a marigold alone meant grief, but combined with roses it expressed the "bittersweets or pleasant pains of love."

In 1835, the anonymous American author of *The Language of Flowers* explained some of the basic grammar rules of florigraphy: "When a flower is presented in its natural position, the sentiment is to be understood affirmatively; when reversed, negatively. . . . The expression of every flower may thus be varied by varying its state or position. . . . The pronoun 'I' is expressed by inclining the symbol to the right, and the pronoun 'thou,' by inclining it to the left." To complicate matters even further, the grammar books did

During the 1800s, books codifying the meaning of flowers were very popular. The drawing shown here and our color illustration, shown opposite, are typical of engravings used in floral dictionaries. The numbers accompanying the flowers referred to a code for the book's language of flowers.

not always agree on meanings or rules, but for the Victorians this mystery only added to the romance of the language of flowers.

While a floral message could be conveyed by simply tucking a single blossom into a letter, Victorians preferred to speak the language of flowers in compact nosegays called tuzzy-muzzies. (See page 61 for information about tuzzy-muzzies.) In May 1855, *Godey's Lady's Book* explained the social importance of preparing tuzzy-muzzies carefully and correctly: "To get a half dozen of mixed flowers bundled together anyhow, and go into good company with such a nosegay in these days, is looked upon as certainly not a mark of high breeding."

Although we no longer exchange tuzzy-muzzies, the language of flowers can still add meaning to the flowers we send. As the author of *The Language of Flowers* wrote, " . . . no spoken word can approach the delicacy of sentiment to be inferred from a timorously offered flower." To help you create your own floral messages, we have culled this flower dictionary from several sources. As you see, some flowers have several meanings and, to avoid misinterpretation, you may want to include a note explaining the language of flowers with your gift!

Dictionary of the Language of Flowers

ACACIA— *Concealed love; beauty in retirement; chaste love; platonic love (from American Indians); symbol of feminist movement*

ACORN—*Life and immortality*

ALYSSUM —*Worth beyond beauty*

AMARYLLIS —*Pride; pastoral beauty; splendid beauty*

AMBROSIA—*Your love is reciprocated*

ANEMONE—*Forsaken*

ANGELICA—*Soaring thoughts*

APPLE—*Temptation*

ARBUTUS—*I love only you; high esteem*

ASPHODEL—*Bearer of regrets, even beyond death; my regrets follow you to the tomb*

ASTER—*Love; daintiness; I share your sentiments; unpredictability*

AZALEA—*Take care of yourself for me*

BACHELOR'S BUTTON—*Single blessedness; celibacy*

BAY—*Glory (used in heroes' garlands)*

BEGONIA—*Beware*

BELLS OF IRELAND—*Good luck*

BITTERSWEET—*Truth*

BLUEBELL—*Humility; constancy*

BOUQUET OF WITHERED FLOWERS— *Rejected love*

CACTUS—*Endurance*

CAMELLIA—*Good luck gift for a man*

   Pink—*Longing for you;* Red—*You're a flame in my heart; unpretending excellence;* White—*You're adorable; perfect loveliness*

CANDYTUFT—*Indifference*

CARNATION—*Fascination; pure love*

   Pink—*I'll never forget you; reciprocated love;* Red—*My heart aches for you; admiration; alas for my poor heart; impetuous love;* Purple—*Capriciousness;* Solid color—*Yes;* Striped—*No; sorry I can't be with you;* White—*Sweet and lovely; innocence; pure love; woman's good luck gift;* Yellow—*You have disappointed me; rejection; disdain*

CATTAIL—*Peace and prosperity*

CHERRY (Pink)—*Good education; good manners and politeness*

CHRYSANTHEMUM—*You're a wonderful friend; cheerfulness and rest; peace in adversity; life; strength of mind*

   Red—*I love you;* White—*Truth;* Yellow—*Slighted love*

CLEMATIS—*Mental beauty*

COLUMBINE—*Folly*

COREOPSIS—*Always cheerful*

CORNFLOWER—*Great happiness*

CROCUS—*Cheerfulness; gladness of youth*

CYCLAMEN—*Resignation; goodbye; diffidence*

DAFFODIL—*You're the only one; the sun always shines when we're together*

DAHLIA—*Pomp; instability; gratitude and good taste*

DAISY—*Innocence; loyal love; I'll never tell; purity. In Middle Ages, daisies on brow meant "I will think of it" if a maiden was unsure of her feelings; on a knight's shield, two daisies meant his love was returned . . .*

DEAD LEAVES—*Sadness; melancholy*

DANDELION—*Faithfulness; happiness; oracle*

FENNEL—*Flattery*

FERN—*Magic; fascination; confidence; shelter;* Maidenhair—*Secret bond of love*

FIG—*Idleness; longevity*

FIR—*Time*

FLAX—*I feel your kindness; domesticity*

FORGET-ME-NOT—*True love; memories*

FORSYTHIA—*Anticipation*

FOXGLOVE—*Insincerity*

FUCHSIA—*Taste; gracefulness; your charms are engraved on my heart*

GARDENIA—*You're lovely; secret love*

GERANIUM—*Stupidity; folly*

   Lemon-scented—*Unexpected meeting;* Ivy—*Bridal;* Oak-leaved—*Warm feelings of friendship;* Dark red—*Melancholy;* Red—*Comfort and consolation;* Pink—*Preference; attention*

GLADIOLUS—*Sincerity*

GLOXINIA—*Love at first sight*

GRASS—*Submission*

HEATHER: Lavender—*Admiration; solitude;* White—*Protection; wishes will come true*

HIBISCUS—*Elegant beauty; transience*

HOLLY—*Defense; domestic happiness; foresight; strength; immortality; aggressiveness*

HOLLYHOCK—*Ambition; fruitfulness*

HONEYSUCKLE—*Generous affection*

HOP—*Injustice*

HYACINTH—*Games and sports; rashness;* Blue—*Constancy;* Purple—*I am sorry; please forgive me; sorrow;* Red or Pink—*Play; pain or sorrow*

HYDRANGEA—*Thanks for understanding*

ICE PLANT—*Your looks freeze me*

IRIS— *Your friendship means a great deal to me; my compliments*

IVY—*Friendship; affection; married love; fidelity*

JASMINE—*Amiability*
JONQUIL—*Love me; desire; sympathy; affection returned*

 LARKSPUR—*Infidelity*
LAVENDER—*Distrust*
LILAC—*First emotions of love*

LILY: Orange—*Hatred*; White—*Virginity; majesty; purity; it's heavenly with you*; Yellow—*I'm walking on air; falsehood*; Calla—*Beauty*; Day—*Coquetry*; Tiger—*Wealth and pride*

LILY OF THE VALLEY—*Return to happiness; sweetness; humility; you've made my life complete*

LOTUS—*I admire you greatly (donor to recipient)*

 MAGNOLIA—*Nobility; love of nature; dignity or perseverance*
MARIGOLD—*Grief; cruelty; jealousy*

MICHAELMAS DAISY—*Afterthought*

MIMOSA—*Secret love*

MINT—*Wisdom*

MISTLETOE—*I overcome difficulties; kiss me; affection; weakness superior to strength*

MONKSHOOD—*Beware, a foe is close*

MOSS—*Maternal love; charity*

MULBERRY—*I shall not survive you*

MYRTLE—*Love; marriage (included in bridal bouquets)*

 NARCISSUS—*Self-satisfaction; inability to love others; stay as sweet as you are*
NASTURTIUM—*Patriotism; victory in battle*

NUTS—*Stupidity*

 OLEANDER—*Caution; diffidence*
ORANGE BLOSSOM—*Innocence; marriage and fruitfulness; eternal love*

ORANGE, MOCK—*Deceit; counterfeit*

ORCHID—*Beautiful lady; love; refinement*

 PALM LEAVES—*Triumph*
PANSY—*Thoughts; remembrance; power of loving thoughts*
PARSLEY—*Rejoice*

PEACH BLOSSOM—*Total devotion and admiration of sender*

PEONY—*Shame; happy marriage*

PETUNIA—*Anger; resentment; I am calmed by your presence; love that cannot be hidden*

PERIWINKLE—*Desire to preserve a sweet memory*

PHLOX—*Unanimity*

PINE—*Hope; pity*

PINEAPPLE—*You are perfect*

PINKS: Clove—*Resignation*; Red—*Pure love*; Striped—*Refusal*

POLYANTHUS—*Pride of riches*

POPPY: Red—*Pleasure; consolation*; Scarlet—*Extravagance*; White—*Consolation; sleep*; Yellow—*Wealth; success*

POTENTILLA—*Maternal love*

PRIMROSE—*Early youth; you are my life*

 RASPBERRY—*Remorse*
RHODODENDRON—*Danger; moment of enchantment, especially first declaration of love*

ROSE: Bridal—*Happy love*; Christmas—*Anxiety; calm me*; Damask—*Ambassador of love*; Dark crimson—*Mourning*; Pink—*Perfect happiness; believe me*; Red—*Love; I love you*; Tea—*I'll always remember*; White—*Innocence; purity; I'm worthy of you; secrecy; silence*; White and Red together—*Unity; England*; Yellow— *Infidelity; jealousy; try to care*; Leaf—*You may hope*; Thornless—*Love at first sight*; Dried white—*I prefer death to loss of virtue*; Withered white—*Fleeting beauty; you didn't impress me*

ROSEBUD—*Youth; beauty; innocence*; Red—*Pure and lovely*; White—*Girlhood*; Moss—*Confession of love; voluptuous pleasure*

ROSES: Bouquet—*Gratitude*; Single bloom—*I (still) love you*; Crown—*Reward of merit*; Wreath in tuft of grass—*Everything may be gained by keeping good company*

ROSEMARY—*Remembrance*

RUE—*Grief*

 SCABIOUS—*Unfortunate love*
SMILAX—*Loveliness*
SNAPDRAGON—*Total indifference*

SNOWDROP—*Hope; sign of life*

SPIDER FLOWER—*Let's elope*

STEPHANOTIS—*Happy marriage; desire to travel*

STOCK (GILLY FLOWER)—*Bonds of affection; lasting beauty*

SUNFLOWER—*Haughtiness; cheerfulness; pride*

SWEET PEA—*Farewell*

SWEET WILLIAM—*Gallantry*

 THYME—*Activity*
TUBEROSE—*Dangerous pleasures*
TULIP—*Perfect love; inconsistency; Holland*; Red—*Declaration of love*; Variegated—*Beautiful eyes*; Yellow—*Hopeless love; sunshine is in your smile*

 VIOLET—*Modesty; humility of giver*; Blue—*Faithfulness; caution*; White—*Let's take a chance*
VISCARIA—*Will you dance with me?*

 WATER LILY—*Purity of heart; chastity; coldness*
WEEPING WILLOW—*Mourning*
WISTERIA—*Friendship*

 YARROW—*War*

 ZINNIA: Magenta—*Lasting affection*; Mixed—*Thoughts or memories of absent friend*; Scarlet—*Dependability*; White—*Goodness*

Wreaths & Decorations

A wreath celebrates the bounty of nature and reflects the personality and individuality of its creator. It is a symbol of hospitality that draws a circle of warmth around family and friends—a circle uniquely yours.

The photos and step-by-step instructions in this chapter show how to create 25 wreaths, garlands, trims and centerpieces suited to all seasons. Here, too, you will find primers on how to preserve fresh flowers by pressing and drying them—even identification guides showing, in color photos, the most common garden flowers suitable for pressing, and 34 dried flower varieties—plus 10 creative projects including wedding momentoes, Easter eggs, a pressed flower valentine and a Victorian topiary.

Wreaths for All Seasons

Make special wreaths for special occasions—or to give as gifts. What could be more charming for a wedding than an all-white dried-flower wreath? Or make a delicate wreath for a baby's christening with baby's breath, lemon thyme to symbolize courage, chamomile flowers to symbolize patience, lavender, mint and statice.

Rose Hip Wreath

Foundation wreath of straw wound with nylon thread
No. 28- or 32-gauge wire
Rose hips, clipped to 3 to 6" lengths
Clippers

1. Tie wire around foundation wreath, forming a loop for hanging.
2. Snip off thorns from rose hips and insert the rose hips in straw wreath, working counterclockwise. This makes a dense and compact wreath that will last for several years.

Dried-Flower Wreath

Foundation wreath (see Hint below)
Dried flowers (see Hint)
No. 28- or 32-gauge wire
Green floral picks
Florist's holding spray or hair spray

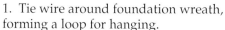 *Foundation wreath may be of straw wound with nylon thread or green Styrofoam. Or try making your own by winding willow branches, honeysuckle vines or grapevines with wire or florist's tape. Flowers to use include lavender, tansy, golden and rose yarrow, feverfew, baby's breath, santolina, hydrangea, blue and white statice, and pink and yellow rosebuds.*

1. Tie wire around foundation wreath, forming a loop for hanging.
2. Make small bouquets of flowers and wrap them with wire. Insert in foundation wreath or anchor to wreath with floral picks. Distribute colors evenly to achieve a balanced effect. Fill in with single dried flowers to cover flower stems.
3. When wreath is complete, take outdoors and spray generously with florist's holding spray or hair spray.

Evergreen Wreath

Wire coat hanger
6 by 12" evergreen sprigs, 24 or more, if needed
Florist's wire
2 yards narrow red or other color ribbon
Pinecones or crab apples
Wire cutters
Scissors

1. Bend the hanger so that it forms a circle, leaving the hook intact.
2. Wire the ends of two or three bunches of sprigs onto the hanger, near the top. Continue wiring bunches onto the hanger frame, making sure they lie in the same direction.
3. When the wreath is finished, snip off protruding ends of the wire and sculpt the wreath's shape by trimming the greens with scissors.
4. Make 12 or 15 small bows and pull a piece of wire through the back of each bow. Attach them to the wreath with the tail ends of wire. You can also attach two or three larger bows instead. Add pinecones or crab apples, if desired, in the same manner.

Victorian Summer

The dried-flower wreath pictured on page 12 is made with 10 hydrangea, 3 large bunches of white baby's breath and 1 bunch of garnet baby's breath (*gypsophilia*), 6 pink delphinium and 8 purple delphinium, 8 large pink roses and 18 small red roses, 10 cockscomb and 6 anise hyssop. Position flowers as shown in photo; alter colors to harmonize with the color of your door.

16" straw wreath form
Dried flowers (see above)
Florist's pins
Glue gun
Florist's holding spray or hair spray
Floral wire, 26-, 27- or 28-gauge

1. Fluff white baby's breath lightly with fingertips to give it fullness if it has been packaged. Make small bouquets of sprigs and, working counterclockwise, attach them with florist's pins to entire top surface of straw form. Overlap bunches to cover ends.
2. Clump three or four hydrangea at the top to form a focal point and space the remaining hydrangea evenly around form. Glue in position.
3. Nestle remaining flowers among sprigs of white baby's breath and glue in place. Take finished wreath outdoors to spray it all over with holding spray.
4. Make a hanger 2 to 2½ inches in diameter by looping florist's wire around four times. Twist ends around loops to secure them. Attach looped wire to top back of form with three florist's pins.

Autumn Bounty

Combining a variety of fruits or other provender in decorative clusters is a style associated with the 15th-century Florentine sculptor della Robbia. By using hollow plastic fruit, sold in craft shops, and an artificial evergreen wreath, you will be able to store your decoration to use another year.

22" artificial evergreen wreath
Large nail; hammer
10 large pieces of hollow plastic fruit
24 small pieces of hollow plastic fruit
Small floral picks

Floral wire, 26-gauge
6 plastic or natural nuts
Glue gun
3 yards of 3"-wide ribbon for bow

1. To attach the large pieces of fruit, punch a nail hole in the back of each piece. Break a floral pick in half and wrap an 8-inch length of floral wire to one end. Drop pick into hole and pull wire so pick catches inside. Position fruit on evergreen wreath as shown in photo. Wrap wire completely around wreath. Twist the end to secure it and trim off any excess wire. Repeat for each piece, leaving an open space at the top for a bow.
2. Position and glue clusters of nuts and smaller fruit in place. Form a bow with the ribbon, and wire it in place at top of wreath. Make and attach a hanger as described in step 4 of *Victorian Summer*.

The effect will be more pleasing if you allow one object to be prominent and coordinate the color of the bow at top with the object. Do not crowd the composition with objects. If necessary, make two different wreaths using favorite toys and collectibles rather than overload one wreath.

Christmas Past

Many of us have a collection of small objects to which fond memories are attached. You might have small decorations and gifts from holidays past. Select a few such objects of personal memorabilia to create a wreath of memories.

18" natural or artificial evergreen wreath
4 yards of 2"-wide floral pattern ribbon
Floral wire, 26-, 27- or 28-gauge
Doll; framed photos and other memorabilia
3 red silk cabbage roses
Shiny objects (crystals, tinsel, beads, etc.)
Monofilament; ⅛"-wide ribbon
Glue gun

1. Use floral ribbon to form a bow as shown in photo and wire it to the top. Use some ribbon to make a doll's skirt.
2. Position a heavy object, such as a doll, off-center inside the wreath near the bottom and wire in place, hiding the wire beneath the clothing. Glue roses in a cluster below the doll.
3. Position framed photos by attaching wire to backs and running wire through or around wreath. Glue on light objects made of paper or fabric, such as the bird and nest, paired on opposite sides.
4. Suspend crystals with monofilament and other hangables, such as keys, with ⅛-inch-wide ribbon. Drape short lengths of tinsel on wreath and glue on beads.

This eye-catching arch of birch twigs welcomes your visitors with a bountiful harvest of the season's best. As long ago as King Arthur's day the British made "kissing boughs" to celebrate the winter solstice holidays. To form those ancient precursors of our modern Christmas trees, they bent twigs of willow into a semicircular arch, then decorated it with

Decorative Doors

greenery, ribbons, apples and little gifts. They hung a sprig of mistletoe from the bottom and suspended the arch from the ceiling in the great hall. Our version celebrates the colorful fall season from the first autumn leaves to the last bite of Thanksgiving turkey. Gourds, if they are cured, will last the season, and then may be stored from year to year.

If you don't have time to dry gourds, use fresh ones or buy artificial pieces from a crafts or gift store. Check fresh gourds often and replace any that show signs of mold or decay. Bring your decoration indoors if a deep freeze is expected; repeated freezing and thawing may ruin the gourds.

12 to 14 small gourds of various types
Household bleach
Soft cloth
Newspapers
Varnish
10"-diameter corrugated wire ring
Brown floral tape
Approximately 100 birch or other wispy branches, 12 to 18" long
No. 23 green floral wire
3 yards burgundy-colored twisted paper ribbon
6 pieces dried strawberry corn
10 ample bunches artemisia with stems approximately 10" long (dusty miller or other filler flowers also work well)
7 stems yarrow
6 burgundy-colored strawflowers
9 golden-yellow-colored strawflowers
6 small bunches purple statice with stems approximately 6" long
Wire cutters
Needle-nose pliers; scissors; pruners
Ice pick or thin knitting needle
Spray fixative or hair spray

Curing Gourds

1. Wash gourds in warm, soapy water and rinse in a solution of 1 part bleach and 4 parts water. Dry each gourd with a soft cloth to avoid bruising or scratching the tender skin.

2. Spread gourds out on several layers of newspaper in a warm, dry, sunny place (a sun porch or a sunny window is ideal) to remove surface moisture. Space gourds apart to allow air to circulate and speed drying. Turn fruits daily; replace dampened newspapers. Let dry in this manner for about one week. Remove fruits that shrivel or develop soft spots to prevent molds and bacteria from spreading to healthy gourds.

3. For final drying, wipe the gourds with a soft cloth soaked in bleach and spread them on newspapers, this time in a warm, dry, dark place. An attic is ideal. Let dry for three to four weeks. Varnish for extra protection.

Making the Arch

1. Cut wire ring with wire cutters. With pliers, bend back each end to form a small loop. Holding each end, stretch wire to a relaxed semicircular arch. To protect hands from wire ends and to make assembly easier, wrap wire arch with brown floral tape.

2. With pruners, cut 8- to 10-inch-long pieces from the tips of the wispy branches. Beginning at the end of the wire arch, attach bunches of twigs (six to eight branches per bunch) to the frame: Wind floral wire tightly around each bunch three or four times to secure.

3. Attach the next bunch of twigs approximately 1 inch above the first bunch; wire securely. Continue in this manner until you reach the center of the frame.

4. Beginning at the opposite end of the arch, attach bunches of twigs in the same manner, until you reach the center again.

Decorating the Arch

1. Make a bow: Untwist the paper ribbon; gather two or three 8-inch loops of paper in your hand. Wire the loops together tightly in the center to form a bow. Wire bow to the center of the arch.

2. Prepare gourds and strawberry corn to be attached: With an ice pick or knitting needle, poke a hole through each gourd near the top. Thread 6 inches of a 12-inch length of wire through the hole, bend, then twist the wire halves together to secure. Cut husks from strawberry corn

and twist wire around the top of each piece where the husks meet the corn.

3. Attach gourds and corn to the arch by twisting their wires around several twigs three to four times. Starting close to the bow, work out and down on both sides, using the photo on page 16 for inspiration. Keep color, shape and balance in mind as you decide on placement.

4. Attach other dried materials and flowers in the same manner, filling in any empty spots to visually soften the piece.

5. Spray arrangement with a fixative or hair spray to protect it. To hang, make a wire loop and attach it to the back of the arch at the center.

If you are careful, your arch will survive the season intact. To store for next year, check the gourds and remove any that show signs of mold or decay. Place the arch in a porous container—perhaps an onion bag—and add a few mothballs. Store in a dry place.

Deck the Door!

When thoughts turn to Santa and gift-laden sleighs, adapt the instructions given here for the Christmas season. Either remove the harvest bounty and replace it with Christmas finery, or make a second birch arch and decorate that. Then deck the door with a Christmas arch reminiscent of its British ancestor, the kissing bough. Don't forget the mistletoe.

A thoughtful door decoration celebrates the season and issues a warm welcome home to family and a cheerful expression of hospitality to friends. Since each season has its own bounty, look for materials that are plentiful. Add a pediment of apples, magnolia leaves or holly sprigs and a pineapple, the traditional symbol of

hospitality, to your door for the winter holidays. Our instructions are for a smaller and slightly simpler version of the lovely pediment capping the door of this 18th-century fieldstone house.

Decor ideas for all the seasons follow. To dry flowers for spring, summer and autumn doors, see pages 40 and 41.

Winter Welcome

½"-thick plywood
Screw hooks and eyes, 3 each
30 eightpenny finishing nails
4 tenpenny finishing nails
Heavy-gauge floral wire
Magnolia leaves or holly sprigs for border
Evergreens for filler: pine or boxwood
30 large red delicious apples
1 large pineapple
Jigsaw or saber saw; ruler; pencil; hammer; staple gun

1. Cut out an arc from the plywood to make a pediment 40 inches wide at the base and 14 inches high at the highest point in the arc.

2. Find the center of your board and trace the outline of your pineapple on the board with a pencil. The pineapple will be impaled on three nails and secured by wiring it to a fourth nail.

3. Screw three hooks into the back of the plywood at the bottom left and right, and center top, about 1½ inches in from edges.

4. Drive 30 eightpenny finishing nails, 3½ inches apart, to make three rows following the arc of the pediment, as shown in the photograph. Drive nails in so that the heads stick out of the plywood at an upward slant for holding the apples. In the same manner, drive four tenpenny nails inside the pineapple's outline for securing the pineapple.

5. Trim bases off leaves. Staple 20 leaves around the top of the board so they protrude 3 to 4 inches. Use two staples to secure each leaf so it won't pivot. Using staple gun, attach sprigs of pine, boxwood or other evergreen to the plywood surface to cover plywood and create background for fruit.

6. Impale an apple on the head of each nail in the arc with stem facing out. Impale pineapple on three bottom nails. Wrap a 12-inch length of wire around pineapple foliage and twist wire around a fourth nail to secure.

7. To hang the pediment over your door, measure and screw eyes into door at position corresponding to hooks. Hang over your door by fitting hooks into eyes. For additional security, wrap 8-inch lengths of heavy-gauge floral wire around each hook and eye.

We've used dried roses, rosebuds and pussy willows to decorate this charming Victorian Spring Bonnet. Cut pussy willows when they first come out, before they turn yellow. If you don't put them in water, they will maintain their just-picked look and can be used in dried arrangements all year long.

Spring Heart with Flowers

12" or 14" heart-shaped wreath, made of grapevine, twigs or straw
Spanish moss
Dried materials: roses; rosebuds; titree; acacia; baby's breath; peppergrass; eucalyptus; boxwood; pussy willow; German statice
2 hummingbird ornaments (blue, yellow)
Ribbon for hanging, about 18"
Florist's wire, about 6"
Glue gun
Super-hold hair spray
Wire cutters

1. Choose a wreath base that is shaped nicely; it doesn't matter what material it is made of because it will be covered with moss and dried flowers.

2. Pull apart the Spanish moss with your hands (it usually comes clumped together tightly) and shape it into a thick line, long enough to cover the base of your wreath.

3. Using the glue gun, draw zigzags of glue on one half of the wreath. (The glue dries fast, so it's best to apply glue in sections.) Attach half of the Spanish moss. Repeat for the second half of the wreath.

4. Using the glue gun, glue the dried flowers and leaves on the wreath, starting with the largest ones. Leave approximately 4 inches between each type of flower. This spacing will give the piece an overall natural effect. Continue adding different materials until you can barely see the moss.

5. Spray the finished piece with super-hold hair spray to help keep it intact.

6. To hang, glue one end of ribbon to center back of top of heart. Tie the ribbon in a bow onto your door knocker. If you don't have a door knocker, slip a 6-inch piece of wire through the back of the bow, twist and make a small loop for hanging.

Fanciful yellow and blue hummingbirds make this floral heart a colorful and lively midsummer door decoration. Feathered friends—hummingbirds and others—are available in crafts shops.

The dried materials suggested here can be augmented with any other flowers, seeds, pods or leaves that are attractive. Try to use a variety of textures and shades of color to make your own wreath unique. If you try to combine too many colors, it may be difficult to create a cohesive design. You might try to focus on a scheme of three colors, accented with different shades of the same three.

Festive Accents

Creating your own decorations is a glorious family tradition to start. The projects here are suitable for everyday decor or festive events. Instructions are simple enough for the whole family to share. If you save those projects completed by the children or grandchildren, they become the best part of your family tradition: They act as memory milestones for the children as they grow up. One evening, spread the dining table with newspapers or an old faded tablecloth, put out materials and share a memory-in-the-making.

Candle Centerpieces

Hollow out green, red and yellow apples, pears and quinces. Place a fat candle in each and arrange as a centerpiece. For spring, place on lemon leaves. In late summer, use huge grape leaves. Evergreens add a seasonal touch for a winter table.

For an amusing autumn centerpiece, hollow out purple and white turnips, kohlrabi, squashes or gourds, or carve a squash basket and place several small candles in it.

Candle Tree

Browse through antique shops for the glass jars with wire loops that were used to light Christmas trees before electricity. They can still be found in old milk glass and pretty colors. Old-fashioned canning jars can also be used. Place small scented candles in jars and hang from the branches of a tree—a quaint, Christmasy decoration for winter, and the perfect lighting for a spring party or summer barbecue.

Apple Bobeches

1 red apple
1 green apple
Juice of 1 lemon
Cloves

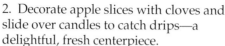

1. Core apples and enlarge holes until apples will fit over a candle. Slice apples ¾ inch thick. Brush both sides with lemon juice or soak in juice for 10 minutes.

2. Decorate apple slices with cloves and slide over candles to catch drips—a delightful, fresh centerpiece.

Herbal Wreath

Instructions for making your own grapevine foundation wreath are in the Hint on page 14.

No. 28- or 32-gauge wire
Foundation wreath of grapevines, honeysuckle or privet
Dried herbs: rosemary, thyme, oregano, marjoram, savory, bayberries, chive blossoms

Tie wire around foundation wreath, forming a loop for hanging. Make bundles of herbs and tie around wreath with wire.

A microwave oven can be used for drying herbs. Place herbs on paper towels and put in oven at lowest heat setting for 2 to 3 minutes. Stir herbs and repeat.

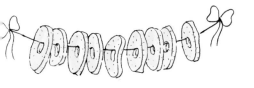

Dried Apple Swags

10 apples: Winesap, Cortland or other winter apples
6 tablespoons powdered ascorbic acid or fruit color preservative
2 qt water
Heavy thread or string

1. Core and peel 10 apples and slice into ¼- to ½-inch rings.

2. Prepare a solution of 6 tablespoons ascorbic acid in 2 quarts water (or prepare solution of fruit color preservative according to package directions). Soak apple slices in solution overnight; drain.

3. Place apple slices on wire mesh in a 250F oven for 4 hours, turning occasionally. Alternatively, place on paper towels and cook 3 minutes in microwave oven at lowest temperature, rotate and cook for another 3 minutes. Air-dry overnight. Thread and hang as swags.

4. For use in cooking, reconstitute apples by soaking in water for 20 minutes or until soft.

Tin Lanterns
Lovely, delicate lighting for an evening meal.

Tinfoil or colored foil
Plastic foam cups
Nail or awl
Small candles

Wrap foil around the inside and outside of a cup, draw a simple pattern on the outside, and punch holes along outline with nail or awl. Insert a small candle.

Spice Wreath

No. 28- or 32-gauge wire
Foundation wreath of grapevines
Spices: cardamom pods; peppercorns; bay leaves; cloves; star anise; cinnamon sticks
White glue

Tie wire around foundation wreath, forming a loop for hanging. Glue small piles of spices to foundation wreath with white glue.

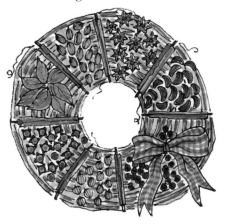

This wreath adds a pleasant spicy fragrance to your kitchen.

Pomanders

Fruits: apples; oranges; lemons; quinces
Spices: cinnamon; orrisroot; whole cloves; allspice
Nail or knitting needle
Ribbon

1. Stud fruits with cloves (use nail or knitting needle to pierce the tough skins of citrus fruits) and roll in ground spices. Different spices complement different fruits. Try these combinations: apples and cinnamon; oranges and orris root; lemons and cloves; and quinces and allspice.

2. Wrap studded fruits with ribbon and use to scent a closet or kitchen.

Here's an idea for using pomanders that makes an unusual wreath: Draw six circles evenly around a 10-inch-diameter foam foundation wreath. Drive three nails through each circle and place clove-studded fruit on the nails. Trim with ribbon or evergreens and hang in the kitchen or dining room.

Bird Feeders

Neighborhood birds will really appreciate this colorful decoration.

Heavy, white cardboard
Waterproof felt-tip markers
6" wooden dowel, ½" wide
No. 28- or 32-gauge wire
¼ cup suet, softened
½ cup birdseed

1. Cut bird shape from cardboard and decorate with markers.

2. Cut a hole in center of bird and insert dowel. Cut another hole and insert wire for hanging.

3. Brush softened suet on both sides of bird tail or wings and press in birdseed.

Tiny Cookie Wreath

Cookie dough or dried peels of lemons, limes and oranges
Tiny cookie cutters
White glue
Small foundation wreath of grapevines

Cut out and bake cookies, using the smallest cookie cutters available. Or cut cookie shapes from dried citrus peels. Glue to foundation wreath.

Pinecones

A handful of small cones and a little imagination are all you need to make Christmas-tree decorations with a country look that will last indefinitely. Since pinecones are notorious dust catchers, seal these ornaments in a bag when you put them away after the holidays.

The mouse (left)—and the turkey inspecting him closely with a corn-kernel eye—are simply pinecones that have been imaginatively transformed with a few bits of felt and ribbon.

A piece of dark cardboard forms an invisible foundation for ornaments made from miniature cones. Create your own shapes: animals, bells, snowflakes, perhaps even a pinecone Santa with a cotton beard and cap.

Pinecone Ornaments

Poster board (for foundations)
**Assorted small and large hemlock cones,
  larch cones and pinecones**
Glue
Clear acrylic spray
Trim for animals

1. To make the wreath, star and candy cane, draw the pattern on a piece of dark poster-weight cardboard and cut it out. Glue small hemlock and larch cones in a regular pattern on both sides of the cardboard. Spray with clear acrylic. Glue a small paper clip at one point for a hanger.

2. To make animals, carefully select pinecones that suggest some characteristic of the animal you wish to make. Trim the main cone with smaller cones, acorns, corn kernels, feathers, berries or pine needles. Pipe cleaners, wire, twigs or branches can be used for legs. Attach a bit of ribbon for a hanger.

This well-constructed pine-cone wreath will add a woodsy warmth to the outside or inside of your home. Hang your wreath unadorned for an autumn-through-late-winter accent; add a jolly red-and-green plaid bow for the holiday season.

Door Wreath

16" tier wire wreath frame
Approximately 5 dozen white pinecones for background
Several large Georgia pine or Norway spruce cones for focal points
Cones of different sizes, such as Scotch, ponderosa, piñon, pitch pine, white spruce, Douglas fir, hemlock, etc.
Florist's wire
Electric glue gun or fast-drying glue
Clear acrylic spray

1. Place wire wreath rounded side down.

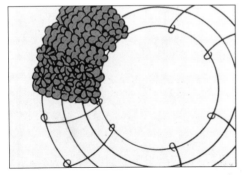

2. Soak white pinecones in water and place them horizontally inside the wire frame with the tip ends, in groups of two or three, in opposite directions. Wet pinecones close but will partially reopen after drying for several days in a warm place, forming a tight, firm base for the wreath.

3. When the base is completely dry, wire large cones to the wreath by circling them with wire, pulling the wires to the back and tying them securely.

4. Fill in areas with assorted cones, using an electric glue gun to secure them. Trim edges with small cones.

5. Spray the wreath with clear acrylic.

Although made of rustic materials, the pinecone door wreath seems to bear a family resemblance to the della Robbia wreaths of the 15th and 16th centuries, which also used natural objects but in a ceramic medium.

Advent Centerpiece

The tradition of lighting a series of candles one at a time on ceremonial days is common to many cultures. The ceremony of marking the progress of Advent is repeated on four succeeding Sundays. The wreath is laid flat as the centerpiece on the dining table or sideboard on the first Sunday in the Christmas season. On that day the family gathers at dusk to light the first candle, to sing Christmas hymns and to read from the Bible. The rose-colored candle is lighted on the third Sunday of Advent, called Gaudete Sunday, as a sign of the joyous season to come.

To make your own Advent wreath, follow the simple instructions here.

After gathering evergreen branches, soak them in water for 8 to 10 hours to clean and thoroughly moisten them. When you are ready to make your wreath, shake excess water off greens before you begin to work.

Evergreen branches
3 pieces sturdy corrugated cardboard, each 11" square
11"-square green felt
4 by 8" piece thin cardboard
Green poster paint
No. 30 florist's wire
Holly and/or pinecones (optional)
1 rose and 3 purple candles, 8 to 10" long
Paintbrush
Pointed tool
White glue; metal ruler; utility knife; scissors; ¾"-wide masking tape; wire cutters; rubber cement

Making the Base

1. Glue three cardboard squares together in layers, with corrugations running in alternate directions.

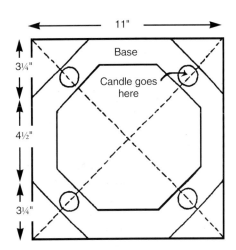

2. With ruler and pencil, draw diagonal lines joining opposite corners of 11-inch cardboard square. From each corner, measure 3¼ inches along both edges and mark those eight points with pencil dots. Join each pair of dots with a ruled pencil line. Using ruler and utility knife, cut away four corners of square along the lines to yield eight-sided figure.

3. Come in 1½ inches from each of eight sides and draw lines parallel to outer edges to mark inner edge of wreath. Use ruler and utility knife to cut out center of cardboard square along these lines.

4. Place cardboard base on 11-inch felt square; draw lines marking outer and inner edges. Using scissors, cut along these lines so felt piece matches base.

5. To position candle holders, mark halfway point (¾ inch) along four diagonals with pencil.

Making the Candle Holders

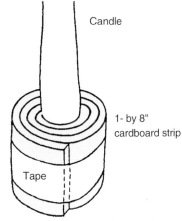

1. From thin cardboard, cut four strips 1 by 8 inches each. Loosely roll strip around base of candle and fasten outside end of strip with 5-inch piece of masking tape. Remove candle and fasten the inside end of the holder with ¼-inch tab of tape. Repeat for three other candle holders.

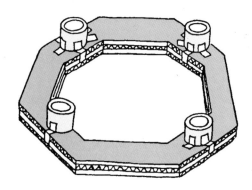

2. Use four 2- by ⅜-inch tabs of tape to secure each holder in place centered over mark on each diagonal. Paint base and candle holders green and let dry.

Attaching the Evergreens

1. To attach evergreens, start by using a pointed tool to poke holes about 2 inches apart over the entire surface of the cardboard base.

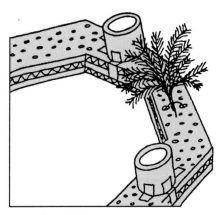

2. Trim evergreen branches to 4 to 6 inches long. Fasten three sprigs together with 20 inches of wire, keeping sprigs flat and leaving two 8- to 9-inch ends of wire. Lay sprigs on base with stems at center and tips pointing toward edges; secure by sticking wire ends through holes and twisting them together at back. Continue in this way with small bunches of sprigs, turning wreath counterclockwise until base is fully covered. Overlap stems with sprig tips if you wish; add holly sprigs using the same wiring method. To add pinecones, attach wires under petals at base of each cone, then push wire ends through holes and twist together.

3. Turn wreath over and cut off all wire ends. Press twisted wires against cardboard and coat back of cardboard with rubber cement. Coat one side of felt with rubber cement, let dry, then press in place against base.

This method of gluing two surfaces together is called "contact cementing" because once the two surfaces make contact with one another, the bond is permanent. To avoid problems, place a piece of paper between the two glued surfaces, line up the edges and then slowly slide out the paper as you press the felt and cardboard together.

Insert candles and your holiday table centerpiece is ready. Misting the wreath every few days will help keep it fresh and green.

Garlands for Special Occasions

A garland enhances the atmosphere of a celebration by carrying a party theme throughout the room. The garland pictured above creates an indoor floral effect for the annual Garden Club Tea. Instructions for making this and other special-occasion garlands follow—including ideas for Fourth of July, a wedding or anniversary and a birthday. Whether draped around a table, a banister or over a doorway, garlands add a memorable touch when friends get together.

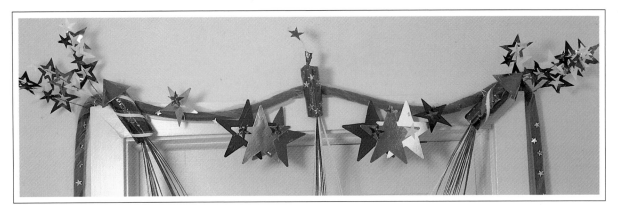

The base material can be welting or cotton clothesline sold at fabric stores. The wrapping is 2-inch-wide strips of fabric or ribbon. To determine the amount of ribbon or fabric strips used in a garland, cut base material to desired length. Cut fabric or ribbon 1½ to 2 times the length of base material. For example, a 4-foot garland uses 6 to 8 feet of fabric strips or ribbon. Glue fabric or ribbon to one end of base with a glue gun. Wrap around base, overlapping slightly to cover completely. Glue end. Glue ribbon accents to one end of base. Wrap, overlapping ¼ inch, or leave opening for spiral effect.

Garden Club Tea

Base material, length of table's
   circumference
2"-wide strips of cream-color fabric
Bunches of purple silk violets
Floral wire
⅛"-wide purple and green ribbons
Glue gun

1. Glue one end of cream fabric strip to end of base. Wrap fabric around base, covering completely. Glue other end.
2. Trim leaves from violet bunches leaving ½-inch stems. Overlap two leaves and wire together. Wire three more leaves, one at a time, to form fan shape. Repeat for desired number of bunches.
3. Wire bunches of leaves to base at even intervals, twisting wire to back. Seal wire ends with glue to prevent them from catching on tablecloth. Glue a bunch of violets to the center of each leaf pattern as shown in photo on facing page.
4. Glue one end of purple and green ribbons to one end of base. Wrap around violet clusters. Glue ends.

Fourth of July

Base material
Blue plastic tablecloth, cut in 2"-wide strips
White tulle
Empty toilet paper rolls
Blue and red metallic tissue paper
½" white tape (at art supply stores)
Self-sticking metallic stars
White-coated floral wire (at florist shops)
White paper; clear tape; string; glue gun

1. Determine length of garland and wrap base with blue plastic strips. Wrap with white tulle to cover blue plastic.
2. For each rocket (see photo above), cut empty paper roll 5 inches long. Cover with blue metallic paper, taping to secure. Cut 2-inch strip of red metallic paper. Tape one end of strip to end of paper roll; wrap in a spiral around roll and tape other end. Spiral white tape centered in red strip.
3. Cut a 4½-inch circle from white paper for rocket top. Cover with red metallic paper. Slit one side of circle to center, then overlap and tape it to form a cone. Glue underside of cone and place on top of paper roll to form nose. Cut thin strips of metallic papers and glue inside base for streamers.
4. Cut empty paper roll 5 inches long for each firecracker. Cover with red metallic paper 2 inches longer than roll. Tape on side. Bring excess paper to the top, adding a heavier piece of string for a wick before excess is tied. Decorate sides with metallic stars.
5. To attach each rocket and firecracker to garland, cut a slit on the back. Knot an 8-inch length of floral wire and slip it into the slit so knot catches inside. Twist ends around base.
6. Cut different sizes of stars from a variety of materials. Glue tips to garland and to each other. Glue clusters of small stars in corners and hang garland on wall.

Wedding Garland

Wire coat hanger for base
Wire cutters
Silk or synthetic lily of the valley
2 yards of ½"-wide green ribbon
4 yards of ⅛"-wide white ribbon
Floral wire, 26-, 27- or 28-gauge
Glue gun

1. Cut a 23-inch length of coat-hanger wire and bend to form an arch around a place setting as shown in photo below. Glue ½-inch-wide ribbon to one end of hanger and wrap completely. Glue end.
2. Glue leaves around entire arch, overlapping each leaf. Glue individual flower sprigs under leaf tips to the stems. Make two bows from ⅛-inch-wide ribbon and tie one on either end as shown in photo.

Here's an idea for a child's birthday party (or an adult's, for that matter): Cut a length of clothesline that can be slung out of reach in an area you want to decorate. Tag a favor with the name of each guest. Use clothespins to attach them to the line, separating each by a balloon. Lower the line when the birthday child opens his or her gifts.

Pressing Fresh Flowers

Pressing fresh flowers removes the moisture, leaving them dry and flat, and preserves their color. There are two simple ways to press flowers. A traditional press, which is especially good for thick petals, dries flowers between layers of blotting paper and corrugated cardboard. These layers are encased between two pieces of plywood held together by screws and wing nuts in each of the four corners. When tightened, the wing nuts apply an even, constant pressure to the flowers. See How To Make a Flower Press on page 29.

If you do not have a press, a telephone book works as well, especially for delicate flowers. A weight, such as a heavy book or a cinder block, placed on top of the telephone book provides enough constant pressure to remove the moisture from the flowers.

A beautiful pressed-flower arrangement depends more upon your selection of flowers than upon your method of pressing. A thick flower, such as a rose, must be taken apart. Lay each petal flat and press the stem, leaves and center separately. After all parts are dry, reassemble them into the likeness of the original flower.

1. Pick flowers late in the morning when they are dry, but before the heat of the day wilts the flowers or bleaches their color.

2. Select flowers and leaves that have pleasing colors, textures and shapes, and no unsightly marks, bruises or other imperfections.

3. Even if you plan to use a press, bring an old telephone book to the garden with you. Place cut flowers between the pages immediately to prevent wilting.

Pressing the Flowers

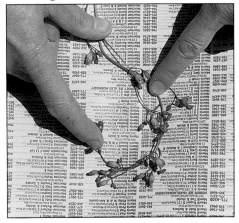

1. *Arrange only a few flowers on each layer of your press or book to allow proper ventilation as the moisture leaves the flowers.*

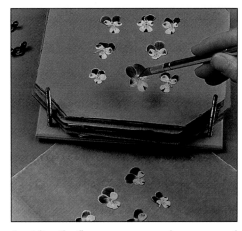

2. *After the flowers are pressed, remove and store them between layers of wax paper in a cool, dry area.*

Predicting How the Colors Will Fade

As the moisture leaves the flowers, their vivid, glossy colors will change to a palette of softer, more muted tones.

Reds will change to deep shades of burgundy or rust; pinks will become coral; and whites will turn ivory.

Yellow and blue flowers usually will retain their colors. Especially striking are the blues of love-in-a-mist, Johnny jump-ups, delphinium and larkspur. Green materials will not change color when pressed but will turn a soft gold when exposed to light.

You can retouch the color of a pressed flower by shaving a chalk pastel of the same color with a razor blade to make colored dust and brushing it onto the flower.

How To Make a Flower Press

Two 10" squares of ¼"-thick plywood with hardwood veneer
Ten 10" sheets of white blotting paper
Six 10" squares of corrugated cardboard
Four 2" round-head stove bolts, ¼" diameter; 8 washers; 4 wing nuts
Pressed flowers
Saber saw or jigsaw; sandpaper; clamp; electric drill with ¼" bit; indelible marker ; white glue; small bowl; small paintbrush; acrylic sealer; scissors

1. With a saber saw, round the corners of the plywood squares. Lightly sand the edges.
2. Measure in ¾ inch from edges at each corner; mark for drilling.
3. Clamp the plywood squares together. Drill a ¼-inch hole at each corner. Use the indelible marker to mark one corner of each square for lining up holes. Remove clamps.
4. Cut blotting paper and cardboard to fit in press. Trim corners diagonally to fit inside the bolts in the press.

Decorating with Decoupage

1. Select pressed flowers and plan an arrangement.
2. Apply a dot of glue to center back of leaves and pressed flowers; gently arrange and press them in place on the top of the flower press.
3. Dilute white glue with a few drops of water in a small bowl or cup. Using the small paintbrush, apply diluted glue to undersurfaces of flower petals and leaves. Carefully press them onto the surface of wood.
4. When glue has thoroughly dried, seal top of press with a thick acrylic sealer, following directions on label.
5. Assemble the flower press with bolts, washers and wing nuts.

Names of flowers, starting upper right, reading clockwise: coral bells, azalea, basket of gold, red and pink verbena, Johnny jump-up, bleeding heart, marigold, columbine and salvia.

Flower Identification Guide

When a flower is pressed, two dramatic changes occur. First, it becomes flat and two-dimensional. Second, with the moisture removed the color of the fresh flower changes, just as the color of most natural objects does when they go from wet to dry. The vivid glossy colors of the petals will be exchanged for a softer palette often associated with the Victorian look. Strong reds will change to burgundy or rust, pinks to coral and whites to ivory. Most yellow and blue flowers hold their color well through the pressing process.

Green grass and leaves get their color from chloro-phyll produced through the process of photosynthesis, which requires moisture and sunlight. When a "green" flower is picked from the garden, the ingredients for photosynthesis are removed so the production of chlorophyll stops. When a leaf is removed from the press, it will still be vividly green, but within 6 months it will often begin to turn a golden brown. In some cases this can actually be quite attractive, but if not anticipated in advance it can spoil the entire look of your arrangement. For this reason be *very* selective in your use of green foliage.

Delphinium
The delphinium family offers the largest spectrum of the color blue from a deep purple to a light blue. Their color has tremendous longevity and goes virtually unchanged for many years. Larkspur, from the same family, has similar characteristics and because of its size can be useful in smaller arrangements.

Columbine
The columbine family has many varied shapes and colors. These flowers should be pressed face down to maintain the design of their inner cone shape.

Fuchsia
To press fuchsia successfully some of the petals must be removed to reduce the density of the flower head. Removing some of the petals also allows for proper air circulation around the flower to ensure the removal of moisture during the pressing process.

Bleeding hearts
Visualize an engraving of an old English garden, and there they'll be in your mind's eye. Their shape and the soft pink of the blossoms lend a romantic quality to whatever arrangement they slide into. The long stems can be formed into gentle curves during the pressing process.

Lobelia

This flower comes in shades of blue, purple and white. Its size lends itself well to small or medium-size arrangements. Its rich blue color lasts for years with barely a change.

Coral bells

The small delicate blossoms and graceful curve of the stem give this flower a lot of versatility. Use it to give a light airiness to an arrangement, or pick it apart and use the tiny blossoms for miniatures.

Johnny jump-ups

These flowers press very well. Choose the ones with darkest, richest colors to get the best results.

It is possible to create more vivid flower colors—even change the colors of the petals entirely—by tinting them with pastel chalk. You can make fine colored powders from colored chalk. Use a single-edge razor blade or craft knife to shave the side of the chalk to create a fine dust. Pick the dust up by dipping the bristles of a small paintbrush into it. Brush the color gently onto the surface of the petals, as you would apply powder to your own nose.

Rather than discard an accidentally damaged specimen of a dried blossom, you may want to set it aside to experiment with the effect that different shades of chalk-dust makeup have on it.

Creating new colors in this way can be fun. However, if you prefer to work only with nature's palette, you should gather and press as wide a variety of flowers as you can so you will have the widest possible variety of colors to choose from when it comes time to create your arrangement.

Marigolds

To press most marigolds successfully the petals must be removed from the dense seed pod and pressed separately. This variety has a much smaller seed pod and can be pressed successfully in full.

Pansies

An old favorite of most flower lovers, the pansy offers a wide range of colors to choose from and is very easy to press.

Verbena

The tiny delicate blossoms work well to accent arrangements and add bits of color here and there. For best results, the flowers must be separated from the head and pressed individually.

Pressed Flower Arrangement, Step-by-Step

Building a basic symmetrical design

1. Pressed floral arrangements are built from the back forward. First define the shape by creating a framework. Plants that have long stems such as coral bells, lavender, salvia or baby's breath work well.

   Mark where the bottom center of the arrangement will be and center the container there. Decide on the height of the space you plan to fill (the size of your finished picture). Glue your first piece of plant material in place in the top center.

   Place the two bottom pieces to right and left of the container approximately parallel with its top opening. Fill the remaining fan shape with corresponding pieces positioned at even intervals.

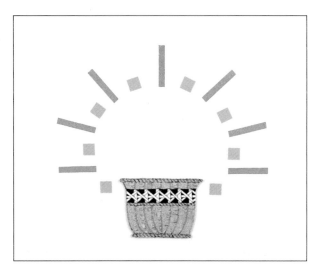

2. Choose plant material that is completely different in size, shape, texture and color from that of the framework to fill in the empty spaces. If you don't have enough of the same flower, you can alternate like flowers, creating a pattern of your choosing. Glue these flowers in place.

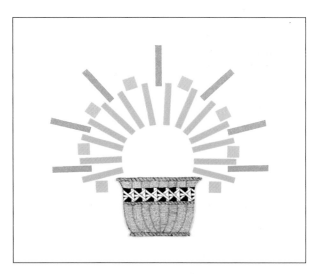

3. Alternate patterns are now being established not only in the framework but in the body of the arrangement as well. As the third layer of the fan is created, use long-stemmed plant material either repeating what was used in the framework or something similar to complement it. Again, if you do not have enough of a single variety of plant to complete this entire layer, create your own alternating pattern with like flowers, then glue in place.

4. Closing in on the center, the fourth layer begins the development of the focal point of your arrangement. Use your brightest and most interesting flowers now. Choose flowers with different shapes and textures from those used in the previous layer.

5. Color and shape are the guidelines for creating the fifth layer. The focal point is now being created, centered above the mouth of the container. A clear plastic graph ruler can be a helpful tool to ensure an evenly balanced placement of your flowers.

6. The final focus of the arrangement is now put in place by gluing a single flower in the open space. Either repeat a flower used in another layer or introduce a new one whose color is complementary to the other flowers in the arrangement.

A Heart of Flowers

Floral designer Suzanne Baybutt created an intricate heart wreath in black, then arranged colorful pressed flowers around it—an original concept with a very Victorian flair. We've provided the wreath on the pattern page to arrange with your own pretty posies.

Create beautiful Victorian flower-pictures by arranging natural pressed flowers into romantic bouquets. Choose colors that match a room's decor and frame them with complementary mats.

11 by 14" white foam-core or mat board
Scissors; pencil; newspapers; tweezers; waxed paper
Spray can of nonyellowing adhesive or white glue
Spray can of nonyellowing clear acrylic spray
Pressed flowers: bleeding hearts; salvia; verbena; larkspur

Finishing and Framing

When finished, set the composition aside to dry about 2 hours. When dry, lay it on newspaper and spray it all over with acrylic sealer following the instructions on the can. Apply at least two coats, allowing each to dry before applying the next. This will keep moisture from discoloring the florals later, even after they are framed.

Suggested mat and frame: Inner mat: ⅜-inch "grey laid," made by Crescent Mat Co. Outer Mat: 2¼-inch (sides and top) and 2½-inch (bottom) "warm white" with black core, made by Bainbridge Mat Co. Frame: ¾-inch red burnished "silver fleck" by Whistler.

1. Cut a piece of white foam-core or mat-board to 11- by 14-inches for the background of your composition. Make a photocopy of the heart-shaped grapevine wreath shown on the pattern sheet.

   Cut closely around the wreath with scissors and center it on the background, marking lightly in pencil where it goes. Spread out some newspapers to catch the spray adhesive in a ventilated area near your workplace. (If you prefer to avoid using sprays, press a dab of white glue on the back of each piece instead of spraying it with adhesive.)

2. Pick up the cutout with tweezers, hold it over the newspaper and lightly spray the back with adhesive. Place it on the background, following your markings to center it. (Once down, it will not peel up without tearing. So start with one corner on the mark and lay it lightly in place.) Smooth it down, working from the center out to the edges to eliminate air pockets that could become wrinkles.

3. Flatten a piece of wax paper over it, so you can see the the graphic design through the wax paper, and tape its corners down if necessary. *Without gluing them down*, start laying out the floral material as shown in the photo. When you are satisfied, remove the tape and gently slide the wax paper off to the side without disturbing the arrangement.

4. You are now ready to begin gluing. If you use spray, hold each piece over the newspaper and lightly spray the back with adhesive before placing it on the background and smoothing or dabbing it gently in place. Follow your pattern because you may tear the pieces if you move them after smoothing them down.

If you use spray adhesive, clean the tips of the tweezers frequently with acetone to prevent the adhesive from building up on them. Read the directions on the spray can to avoid overspraying or clogging the nozzle. When the composition is complete, clean your hands thoroughly with the cloth soaked with acetone.

5. Build up the arrangements in layers. First, glue the bleeding hearts in place as shown. Their stems blend with the grapevine nicely.

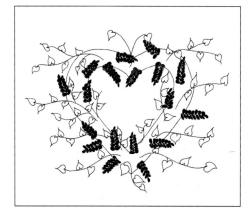

6. Layer the blue salvia on top of the bleeding hearts, distributed evenly around the wreath, but not perfectly symmetrically.

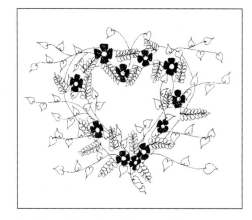

7. Place the red verbena as shown. Distribute blue larkspur between the verbena blossoms, allowing some to overlap.

Elegant Eggs

This project shows how to create exquisite decorations by applying pressed flowers to a delicate blown-out eggshell and decorating it with ribbons. The ribbon loop attached to the top will allow your egg to adorn a wreath, a springtime tree at Easter or a traditional Christmas tree. Handmade ornaments like these can become part of a seasonal family tradition if they are wrapped and stored carefully. They may even become cherished heirlooms, passed down through the family from one generation to the next.

Before beginning this project, see pages 28 and 29 for instructions on drying and pressing flowers and foliage. Spray adhesive and acrylic spray fixative are available at art supply and craft shops.

Clean, white eggs
Hat pin or large needle
Small bowl
Pressed flowers and leaves
Pencil and sheet of white paper
Tweezers
Spray adhesive
Clear acrylic spray fixative
2' of ¼"-wide ribbon for each egg
Craft glue

The color scheme of your arrangement will be most appealing if you select dried, pressed flowers and leaves that share similar color tones, or if you reproduce color combinations as they are found in nature.

Blowing Out the Egg
Blowing out eggs is an old-time skill you may already know, but in case you don't . . .
1. Let the egg warm to room temperature. Use the hat pin or needle to punch a ⅛-inch-wide hole at one end of the egg. Punch a slightly larger hole at the other end of the egg.

2. Insert the hat pin into one of the holes to pierce and agitate the yolk until it begins to break. Place a small bowl on the counter to collect the contents of the egg. Place your mouth over the smaller hole and blow hard enough so the yolk and white run out through the larger hole on the other end and into the bowl.
3. Rinse out the empty eggshell by filling it with water and shaking it gently. Blow the water out of the eggshell in the same way as before. Refill the eggshell with water, shake and blow it out again. Set the emptied eggshell upright in an egg carton or in a cup to drain dry overnight.

Attaching the Floral Elements
1. Once you have glued the delicate floral elements, they are almost impossible to remove intact, so work out your arrangement first by laying out the pressed elements on white paper. When you have an arrangement you like, draw around the flowers and leaves with a pencil; slide the pieces aside and label the drawn outlines with their names and colors.

2. When the eggshell is dry, pick up a flower with tweezers, starting with the bottommost one if the elements in your design overlap. Turn the flower over and lightly spray adhesive on the back, holding the nozzle about 8 inches away. Using your tracing as a guide, place the flower in position on the surface of the egg. The spray adhesive dries very quickly, so place the flower as precisely as possible.

3. Allow the glue to harden overnight. Seal the entire surface of the decorated egg with three light coats of clear acrylic spray fixative. Follow directions on the label to avoid sags. Allow the spray to dry completely between coats.

Attaching Ribbons
1. Measure and cut a length of ribbon to wrap around the height of the egg, as shown. Spray the back of the ribbon with adhesive and wrap it around the egg so the ends meet at the top.
2. Cut an 8-inch length of ribbon for the hanging loop. Overlap the ends slightly and glue them to the top of the egg. For maximum strength use craft glue rather than spray adhesive.
3. Cut a 5-inch length of ribbon for the bow. Loop it and glue the ends and center of the loop to the top of the egg, hiding the ends of the hanging loop.

Desk Set

Making a collage of dried flowers has the same elements as any craft: Gather the raw materials, prepare them, plan the design, assemble the elements, finish for display or use. The artistic statement can be as simple as one flower or as complex as an arrangement of fresh flowers

How To Arrange a Design

Start with the size of the space your design must fit into. A painting can be any size you like (but if you want to frame it, use standard frame sizes). Then ask yourself what colors you want to let dominate, to fit into the decor of a room, for example. Then lay out the work-surface material you will attach your design to. Plain white watercolor paper is a good work surface to start a painting.

If you are partial to Victorian tradition, perhaps a lace border and a traditionally feminine tuzzy-muzzy would make up into a pretty display. When you use flat, dried flowers to interpret a miniature full-blown nosegay (with the stems bound in a long-legged ribbon), you just "paint" it in place on the page. Show only the petals, leaves and stems you would be able to see if someone held it up in front of your face so you could view it at eye level. Start from the center and work out on both sides to the outer edge of the nosegay. Cut a real satin ribbon (rose is a pretty color) and arrange it flat as if it were tied around the stems. Put a border of lace (a paper doily will do) behind the paper surface you have arranged your flower painting on. Then frame it with cardboard behind and glass in front.

Line Material is used to define thin and graceful lines (colorless grasses or ferns are good). They are gathered at the bottom and spread outward, like the veins in a leaf, to the very top and outer sides of your design. They are only a skeleton to give the flowers a frame to live in comfortably.

The Picture is a flat flower arrangement. Slip the dried flowers onto the work surface and, with tweezers or gentle fingers, arrange them into a bouquet. Its outer limits can't go beyond the line material. Cluster the flowers along the line material as if those lines were a weak magnet. When you are happy with the arrangement, make a mental note or a light pencil outline around them. You may have to disturb them to establish a base at the bottom of the composition you have created.

Base Materials are usually ferns or leaves. They are thick solids on which the excitement of the painting comes home to rest. Spread them sparingly across the bottom of the composition, as if they were the earth it grew out of. But curl them upward at the ends because they are not dead; they are graceful, living participants in your composition. Mark their positions with memory or pencil.

How To Attach the Elements

Start with the line material because it should recede into the background. Put a dab of glue on the back of it in enough spots to hold it flat. A toothpick will drip a small enough portion if you dip it into a puddle of glue.

When the lines are "drawn," put a dab of glue on the back of each flower or petal and assemble the picture, following your outline.

Lay the base in place with dabs of glue, following your plan. (Or change it at the last minute to make it better!)

Background Materials and Coatings

Dried plant materials can be glued to any surface glue adheres to. Or an arrangement can be captured, immobile for generations, on a stiff surface covered with glass. Some simple flower shapes define their essence best on black velvet; others on plain paper framed with a tinted mat. If you glue your composition onto glass, consider painting the back of the glass pane in a shade that gathers, but doesn't compete with, the colors of the flowers.

In the old days, the flowers were arranged with no coating; but glass or an acrylic spray or brushed coating, gently applied, can preserve the composition and be easier to dust.

Projects Shown

The parts to make the lamp (shown opposite) are stocked by craft shops in kit form. The floral arrangement was composed on the translucent panels, each panel was covered with a clear protective sheet and the panels assembled.

The pencil cup is a shelled-walnuts can wrapped in a muslin-like, pale yellow fabric to which the dried flowers had been applied. The fabric was then wrapped around the can, covered with a contact-adhesive, clear vinyl sheet, and the edges trimmed with real velvet ribbon.

The address book was covered with fabric glued permanently in place. The flower composition was glued in place on the cover. Then, again, it was covered with a commercial, contact-adhesive, clear vinyl sheet.

The note paper is the most pure and simple. The dried flowers were glued onto a sheet of nice paper that had matching envelopes, then coated with a piece of waxed paper, cut to fit and applied with a warm iron.

The arrangement of flowers on the top surface of the flower press pictured on page 29 was covered with a fast-buildup, super-thick, acrylic sealer sold in craft stores. It simulates, in one coat or two, the many, many layers of traditional clear finishes necessary to build a flat, protective surface.

Other Project Ideas

Glue flowers onto the back of transparent glass tiles, then mount them around a fireplace or kitchen counter.

To make a window lite, sometimes called a "suncatcher," glue a floral composition between two layers of clear glass. Hold them together with tape around the rim or join them with lead cames (lead rods used for leaded window panes), soldered together.

Wouldn't a white wicker breakfast tray be pretty with an array of pressed flowers and a border of ferns or real lace beneath the glass? The same technique could work for a vanity table.

Drying Fresh Flowers

The art of displaying dried flowers as a tasteful element of room decor depends, in part, on the craft of gathering them and protecting their delicate shapes and colors. See pages 42 to 45 for guidance in arranging dried flowers; see page 41 for ways to preserve them. You can buy dried flowers from a florist or craft shop, of course, but you'd be missing out three ways: first, a wonderful excuse for long walks in the fields and forests each season of the year; second, an opportunity to work the colors and fragrances of your natural surroundings into your interior decor; and third, the pride and economy of learning and perpetuating skills that have brought pleasure for generations.

Collecting nature's bounty of ingredients for dried-flower arranging is a year-round project. Each season contributes interesting materials to the cornucopia; these should be gathered as they become available throughout the year.

When selecting types of flowers to dry, remember:

Results are best if the head is not heavy and the stem is not thick. Pick them before they are fully mature; otherwise, they may shed petals as they dry.

Some types that dry well include blue salvia, globe amaranth, tansy, catananche, cockscomb, statice, globe thistle, artemisia and pearly everlasting.

Common flowers that retain their color and shape well are larkspur, red salvia, marigold, zinnia, ageratum and old-fashioned cabbage rose.

Many pinecones will be ready for collection in midsummer when they drop off the trees; these should be gathered while their beautiful tan and brown colorings are strong and fresh and not yet spoiled by contact with the ground.

Leaves of palmetto, seagrape, eucalyptus and mullein can be dried in their natural form.

Fern fronds are collected in the late summer before they curl and shrivel. They should be pressed flat between sheets of newspapers weighted with stones and boards.

Decorative gourds are best harvested before the first frost in the fall hits the garden. They should be washed and dipped in household disinfectant before drying them on layers of news-paper in a warm, dry place. Rotate the gourds often to ensure even drying.

Regardless of the drying method used, the colors may change. White and yellow flowers hold their colors well, but red, blue and pink flowers tend to fade. Avoid overdrying any petaled flowers.

Methods for Drying Flowers

Hanging Method: Your "drying room" should be dark (so colors won't fade as fast), dry and cool (but no less than 50F), with good air circulation. Affix a pole or wire to hang the flowers from, preferably about 6 inches from the ceiling to allow adequate ventilation for the stems. Prepare your flowers by removing lower leaves and thorns, then tie loosely in groups of five or so using string. Spread the blossoms out as much as possible to facilitate airflow among them (they may rot if they are too close together). Hang them upside down from your pole or wire with about 10 inches between the bunches.

Cornmeal-Borax Method: Almost any flower can be dried in a mixture of cornmeal and borax. One part borax to three or four parts cornmeal is usually recommended. The mixture should be stirred very well to remove any lumps. Select a sturdy open container, a box or pan, of a size that will accommodate your flowers (often an old shoe box works well). Spread 1 inch of the cornmeal-borax mixture in the bottom of the container, lay the flowers on top, then carefully sift more mixture around the flowers until they are covered. Put the container in a warm place for 1 to 3 weeks until all moisture is removed. The cornmeal-borax mixture will prevent the flower petals from withering while they are drying.

Granular substances prevent the petals from withering while they dry. In the old days, fine-grained sand was used.

Flat-faced flowers should be placed face down in the mixture, while fluffy flowers should be placed face up. Make sure none of the flowers touch each other. If you use a pan instead of a box, you can put the pan in a warm (200F) oven for several hours and speed up the drying process.

Silica Gel Method: Some prefer to use silica gel in place of the cornmeal-borax mixture, as it is much faster and the blossom colors are more likely to hold true. Silica gel is available at most florist and garden shops and, although costly, can be reused almost forever. If you use silica gel, follow the directions for the cornmeal-borax mixture, but be sure to check the flowers after 48 hours. When flowers are dry, they can be very carefully removed and will be quite natural in shape. Handle them carefully, using a watercolor paintbrush to remove drying material.

Store them in plastic bags or tightly covered containers after they are dry, as humidity will spoil them.

After the flowers are arranged in a bouquet, spray the arrangement with a clear plastic. A dull, clear spray, available in hardware and paint stores, is the least expensive, but you can even use hair spray if you wish. The spray gives strength to the papery-dry petals and protects them from humidity.

(To press flowers, see page 28.)

Dried Flower Arrangements

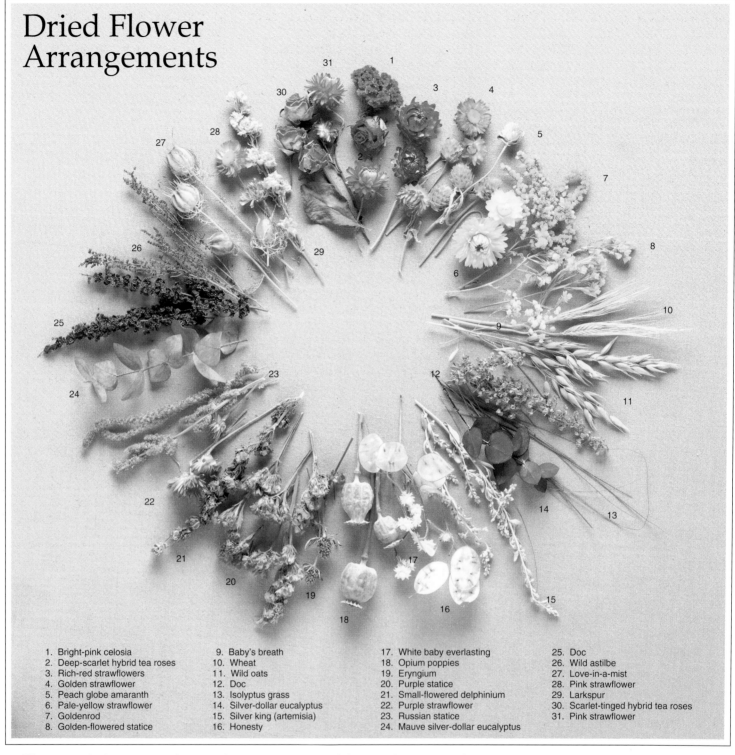

1. Bright-pink celosia
2. Deep-scarlet hybrid tea roses
3. Rich-red strawflowers
4. Golden strawflower
5. Peach globe amaranth
6. Pale-yellow strawflower
7. Goldenrod
8. Golden-flowered statice
9. Baby's breath
10. Wheat
11. Wild oats
12. Doc
13. Isolyptus grass
14. Silver-dollar eucalyptus
15. Silver king (artemisia)
16. Honesty
17. White baby everlasting
18. Opium poppies
19. Eryngium
20. Purple statice
21. Small-flowered delphinium
22. Purple strawflower
23. Russian statice
24. Mauve silver-dollar eucalyptus
25. Doc
26. Wild astilbe
27. Love-in-a-mist
28. Pink strawflower
29. Larkspur
30. Scarlet-tinged hybrid tea roses
31. Pink strawflower

One of the nicest things about working with dried flowers is there are no hard and fast rules to contend with. It seems as though every time someone comes up with a definite rule, someone else finds a wonderful way to break it. The colors are softened by the drying process so it is very hard to find combinations that truly clash. Some of the most dramatic and most beautiful arrangements have been made from contrasting colors: blue and pink, green and orange, purple and yellow.

When choosing your colors, think about the feeling you want your arrangement to convey. Should it be dramatic, festive or country? Select the bright colors first, in shades to complement the surroundings, and select the other flowers and grasses to concur.

Choose the softer pastel shades for a more subtle, romantic mood.

One glance at these two arrangements illuminates the idea; they are basically the same in design but drastically different in color—and humor. Which one would feel best in *your* favorite room?

As you begin to build the arrangement, imagine a fan shape with the biggest, brightest flowers in the middle. Try to follow nature: Trees are heaviest at their base and reach out and up with smaller and smaller branches. Instructions for arrangements begin on page 44.

Victorian Pastel Arrangement

10 silver-dollar eucalyptus
12 stems silver king (artemisia)
15 baby's breath (mini gypsophila)
5 German statice
5 deep-scarlet hybrid tea roses
5 opium poppies
3 bright-pink celosia
25 Russian statice
10 purple statice
5 white baby everlasting
20 small-flowered delphinium
20 larkspur
10 pink xeranthemum
10 purple xeranthemum
5 honesty branches
15 pink strawflowers
20 stems wild oat

Autumn Harvest Arrangement

8 mauve spiral eucalyptus
12 stems silver king (artemisia)
12 stems golden (glycerine) baby's breath
12 groups of lonas
5 deep-scarlet hybrid tea roses
4 yellow strawflowers
3 pale-pink celosia
8 stems goldenrod
7 tansy (also called button yarrow)
6 groups peach globe amaranth
30 stems isolyptus grass
12 stems doc
2 deep-rust strawflowers
4 scarlet-tinged yellow strawflowers
8 stems wheat

We used the materials listed here. For information on collecting your own, see page 41.

To Assemble Either Arrangement

13 by 5 by 6"-high basket with one flat side or other container suitable for hanging on the wall

13 by 5 by 6½" block of dry florist's foam (it should fit the basket tightly and be ½ to 1" taller)

Spool of medium-gauge wire

6 by 6" area of sheet moss or Spanish moss (enough to cover exposed sides of foam)

30 wired picks, 2 to 5" long (see Hint at right), available at most florists

Green florist's tape (see Hint at right)

Wire cutters; sharp knife; can of spray fixative or hair spray

If the stems of your flowers are very brittle (they break easily when you insert them in the florist's foam), attach the stems to wired picks, then cover the picks with green florist's tape. Don't be tempted to use plastic foam in place of florist's foam because fragile stems will break more easily.

1. Cut the foam block with the knife to fit the container tightly, then set block in basket. Place moss only on exposed sides of block. Keep top of block free of moss—stems will cover it completely.

2. Cut a piece of wire 36 inches long. Thread the wire through the back of the basket. Wrap the wire completely around the moss and the foam block, then tie the wire ends together. If your container is solid, crisscross two pieces of masking or florist's tape across the foam to hold it securely to the container.

3. Lay all your flowers out on a table, as shown on page 44, or on the floor so you can easily reach them. Stabilize your container in a spot where you must look up at it—ideally, where your arrangement will be placed when completed. (If you look down on it while working, stems may show more prominently than you would like when it is viewed from below.)

The following instructions are for the Victorian arrangement, with those for the Harvest arrangement in parentheses.

4. Make a skeleton of the arrangement's shape by setting highest and widest points with silver-dollar eucalyptus and silver king (mauve spiral eucalyptus and silver king) to frame the arrangement and draw the eye outward. The arrangement's height should be 1 to 1½ times the container's height. Add some fillers, mini gypsophila (baby's breath) and German statice (lonas), making sure to set some way down deep to help hide your florist's foam block.

🌀 *Don't hesitate to drape your flowers over the container's edge—your result will look more professional if you do.*

5. Place brightly colored focal-point flowers next to be sure they have enough space and prominence. Use deep-scarlet hybrid tea roses (deep-scarlet hybrid tea roses) and opium poppies (yellow strawflowers). Place bright-pink celosia (pale-pink celosia) in the lower center and Russian statice (goldenrod) to frame the celosia.

Insert smaller, softly colored flowers, purple statice and baby everlasting (tansy and peach globe amaranth), throughout the framework. Add more long, lean flowers, small-flowered delphinium (isolyptus grass) and larkspur (doc), to reach outward and further delineate the arrangement's shape. Stay within your original skeleton, but let the flowers take different heights. The in-and-out effect of varied depth creates an airy feeling.

6. Highlight these lean flowers by inserting more interesting color among them with pink xeranthemum (deep-rust strawflowers) and purple xeranthemum (scarlet-tinged strawflowers). In the Victorian arrangement, also add honesty and pink strawflowers. Again, vary lengths of flowers for an "in and out" natural, airy look. To enhance the feathery appearance, add wild oats (wheat) evenly throughout the arrangement.

7. Spray your finished arrangement with fixative or hair spray to help protect it from humidity.

🌀 *If your arrangement has not taken a nice shape, touch it up by adjusting the height of any flowers and/or rounding it out with more filler flowers, using baby's breath (mini gypsophila).*

Bridal Memories

When a dear friend marries, her closest friends will want to celebrate with her and remind her how cherished she is. A wonderful way to make the memories of her wedding day last is to preserve the bride's bouquet and present it to her in a lovely shadow box—a reminder that, with a little effort, both friendship and flowers can last long after the wedding day.

This is the original wedding bouquet that was recreated in the shadow box on page 46.

The fresher the flowers are when you start, the better they will dry, so arrange beforehand for the bride to give you her bouquet immediately after the ceremony. Place the bouquet on a tray in a cooler of ice, making sure the ice does not come in contact with the flowers. This will keep the bouquet fresh until you get it home. If you won't be attending the ceremony, have the bride arrange with someone to do this step for you.

Bouquet of flowers
Silica gel
Airtight container large enough to accommodate all flowers and silica gel
4 to 5"-deep shadow box, large enough to accommodate the bouquet plus at least 2" on each side
Enamel paint, glossy or flat black or shade to match wall where box will be displayed
1 yard velvet fabric in color to complement colors in bouquet
Spray-type mounting adhesive
Large tray
Clear acrylic spray
Clear silicon glue
3" plastic foam ball
Picture frame, dimensions to fit shadow box
Glass, dimensions to fit picture frame
6 small screw eyes; 4 small screws
Picture-hanging wire, 1½ times width of shadow box
Small paintbrush; ruler; scissors; screwdriver

Ready-made shadow boxes are available unfinished in many sizes at craft and hobby stores. Purchase one large enough to accommodate the bouquet plus at least 2 inches on all sides. Use a shadow box with dimensions to fit a standard-size picture frame to minimize the expense.

Drying the Bouquet

1. Take a photograph or make a good sketch of the bouquet before dismantling it so you can easily reassemble it accurately.

2. Carefully take the bouquet apart and follow instructions for drying flowers with silica gel on page 41. You may cut most of the stems off the flowers as they won't be needed later. Save any "extras" from the bouquet, such as ribbons and lace netting, to use later. For appropriate drying time for the flowers you are working with, refer to the label on the silica gel can.

Preparing the Box

1. Ready-made shadow boxes are usually made of plywood. It's important to finish the box carefully so that it will look pretty when viewed from the side. Paint with enamel paint following manufacturer's instructions. Let dry; apply a second coat of paint.

2. Line inside of box with velvet. Cut fabric pieces to appropriate size and shape, then spray back of fabric with mounting adhesive. Press in place and smooth out any wrinkles, making sure material meets neatly at all corners.

Reassembling the Bouquet

The reconstructed bouquet will be about half the size of the original.

1. Remove flowers from silica gel when dry. Brush silica gel mixture from flowers very gently with small paintbrush and set flowers onto a tray. If any petals drop off, set them aside; they will be used later in reconstruction. Be sure to remove any traces of silica gel. Separate flowers into groups of each variety and separate the best of each group from the others. (You may not need all the flowers, so be sure to use the best ones first.)

2. Spray each flower individually with clear acrylic spray. This enhances color and stability.

3. If any lace or netting was used in the original bouquet, gather it together into a circle. Center inside the shadow box and affix with clear silicon glue. If no netting or lace was used, go to step 4.

4. Cut 3-inch plastic foam ball in half and glue on top of netting or in center of shadow box.

5. To attach flowers, place a dab of silicon glue onto plastic foam ball, then press flower in place. Begin assembly with largest flowers first, leaving room around them to fill in with smaller flowers. Foliage and baby's breath are added last. Attach extra petals wherever needed by placing them right into a dab of silicon glue.

6. If bouquet has a bow, attach in place with silicon glue.

Framing the Shadow Box

1. Clean glass well on both sides. Place glass into picture frame. Lay shadow box face down on top of glass, inside frame.

2. Screw one screw eye into each side of back of picture frame. Once screw eyes are in place, thread a screw through each screw eye and mount into shadow box. Connecting the frame to the shadow box this way allows for easy access into the shadow box later, if necessary.

3. Attach two screw eyes into back of shadow box, close to the edges, for hanging wire. Be sure not to insert too deep. Thread wire through and wrap securely at each end.

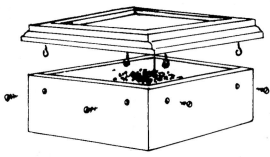

Topiary Technique

For centuries gardeners with a flair for the dramatic have practiced topiary art, trimming and training living ornamental trees and shrubs into fascinating shapes. Our miniature indoor topiary, reminiscent of its early origins, has a natural-branch trunk and a colorful mix of dried-flower foliage. Display this easy-to-make accent solo or in pairs on a mantel or sideboard. Choose an interesting container, such as a blue-and-white oriental-style pot or a colorful glazed ceramic pot. You can use a simple clay gardening pot and dress it up with a little paint: Mist the pot lightly with spray paint, sponge it with acrylic or latex paint (watered down) or paint it a solid color. Try using an old mossy clay pot for an informal straight-from-the-potting-shed look.

The instructions here are for a topiary the size of the one shown opposite—18 to 20 inches high, depending on the branch stem you use. To follow rules of proportion, use a plastic foam ball that is the same diameter as your container. Make the height of your topiary trunk and foliage five times the height of your container. You may substitute other dried materials for those suggested here to suit your container or decor.

Size ratio:

5

to

1

Equal diameter

15" section of branch approximately
   ¾" diameter
4"-diameter clay pot
Florist's or masking tape
¼ block of dry florist's foam
Plaster of paris
Green sheet (sphagnum) moss
4"-diameter plastic foam ball
12 to 15 moss pins or wire bent into
   U-shapes
1½ yards of ½ to ¾"-wide ribbon or lace
   for bow
Wire for bow
Dried materials (approximate amounts):
   8 pieces reindeer moss
   45 stems pink globe amaranth
   15 stems purple statice
   15 stems rose-color strawflowers
   6 stems echinops (globe thistle)
   8 pieces tree moss
   10 stems ageratum
   8 stems sea lavender
   1 large head pink hydrangea
   24 leaves lamb's ears
   9 small pieces celosia (cockscomb)
Pruning shears or crafts scissors
Large knife (to cut florist's foam)
1-qt disposable container and
   spoon for plaster
Hot glue gun and glue sticks
Surface sealer or hair spray

Preparing the Trunk

1. Use pruning shears to cut and trim your branch to size.

2. If your pot has a drainage hole in the bottom, tape over the hole from inside the pot to prevent leakage of plaster. Cut a block of florist's foam about half the height and close to the width of the inside of the container. Insert the trunk into the foam and place it in the pot. The foam holds the trunk in place while the plaster sets, and it also contracts to provide space for the plaster to expand without cracking the container.

3. Add about 1 cup of water to 1 cup of dry plaster a little at a time, mixing until you have a thick, pourable consistency. Pour the plaster into the pot within ½ inch of the pot rim. Plaster sets fast, so work quickly. Turn the pot in all directions to even out the plaster and position the branch as desired in the container, then press sheet moss into the wet plaster surface to cover plaster. Let the plaster dry for at least 1 hour.

Adding the Foliage

1. Using the hot glue gun, apply glue to the top 2 inches of the trunk. Position and push the foam ball firmly down onto the glued portion of the trunk. Using moss pins, pin sheet moss to the surface of the ball to cover completely.

2. Make a bow with the ribbon; secure the bow at its center with wire. To attach the bow, insert the wire into the base of the foam ball where it meets the trunk.

3. Beginning at the base of the foam ball, hot glue small pieces or clusters of your chosen dried material, inserting stem ends into the moss.

4. Arrange the groups of material evenly over the ball surface. Make sure some material protrudes slightly to give the topiary a more natural appearance.

5. Spray the entire surface with a surface sealer or hair spray to preserve your work and protect it from dust.

Fragrances & Floral Designs

To capture the perfume of the summer season for yearlong pleasure, try making potpourris and sachets to scent closets and drawers and to ornament your bureau; or share the enjoyment of gifts with that special homemade touch by giving them to family and friends.

Choose among 37 gifts and decorative accents for the home, using traditional floral designs and techniques. Here you will learn how to fashion a bride's necklace of beads made from the crushed petals of rambler roses, bake spicy trims for a holiday tree, and concoct natural fragrances for the bath. You can select from floral baskets and bows, pierced lamp shades, classic theorem painting on velvet, and a luscious cabbage rose in needlepoint. Though the materials lists are complete and instructions detailed, they are set up so you can easily change the colors to match your own decor.

Potpourris

Cornflower, delphinium, zinnia, peony, strawflower, chrysanthemum, marigold and rose, among others, make beautiful bouquets or can become fragrant potpourris and sachets.

"Potpourri" is a French word meaning mixture, such as a medley of songs, a meat stew or, in this case, a pot of dried and preserved flower petals, leaves, seed berries and roots, tempered and preserved with oils and spices. The mixture is placed in a perforated container or, better, a transparent, open-topped jar to let you see the rich, subtle colors as well as smell the lovely fragrance, which acts as a natural freshener.

"Sachet" is a potpourri mixture tied usually in a little muslin bag and placed in a drawer or closet to scent clothing and linen. A very fine lace is pretty for a sachet but will allow the dried petals to sift through as they crumble unless they are first contained in muslin. The traditional sachet shape is a gathered bag, but a teddy bear makes a charming notion for a child's drawer.

There are as many potpourri recipes as there are fragrances, some of which contain exotic ingredients. However, our potpourri is a simple one that you may vary to suit the combinations of flowers and spices you have to work with or whatever scent makes your nose twitch with pleasure.

1 qt flower petals
1 oz spices, such as clove, nutmeg, mace, cinnamon or allspice
1 oz fixative, such as powdered orrisroot, tonka bean, calamus, dried ground citrus peel, angelica root or gum benzoin
Oil, such as oil of rose, oil of lavender or other aromatic oils available from druggists
Salt (optional, for drying)
Net, lace or muslin (for sachets)

Drying the Petals

Pick petals from flowers that are about to bloom; their fragrance will last longer. Try roses, carnations, geraniums, honeysuckle, lavender, lilacs and perhaps a few leaves of herbs, such as mint or rosemary.

There are *two* drying methods:
1. Spread petals out in a dark, airy room. If you turn them over every day or so, they will dry completely in about a week.
2. Put about an inch of salt in cake pan and place petals on top; sprinkle lightly with salt until completely covered. Put pan in sun for several days, or put in oven under low heat for an hour or two. (The heat speeds up the absorption of the moisture in the petals by the salt.) When petals are dry, remove them from the salt and store them in airtight containers.

Preparing Potpourri

1. Grind spices and fixative to a coarse powder in a mill or with a mortar and pestle. Add a few drops of oil and mix together; smell mixture and add oil sparingly until the odor pleases you. Store mixture in an airtight container for a week or two.

2. Add spice-and-oil mixture to the dried petals, stirring gently with a wooden spoon. Place finished potpourri in a perforated container or glass jar. To make a sachet, place about ½ cup potpourri in a small net or lace bag and tie or sew the opening closed.

Sachets

Bustles. Lace fichus. Cartwheel hats. High fashion to the Victorian lady, but hardly compatible with the briefcase, tennis shoes or coveralls of today's woman.

What to do, now that romantic dress is back? Be authentically (but comfortably) Victorian with a secret sachet—worn hidden under your clothes, the warmth of your body releasing its fragrance.

If you were looking for lace to make a secret sachet in 1886, you might have ordered the piece above from the Bloomingdale Brothers' Catalog. You could have made a Victorian lace fichu like one pictured to the right, and then used a scrap to make a secret sachet. For today a thoughtful idea is to retrieve the bridal bouquet to make a sachet as a permanent memento of the wedding—for yourself or as a gift to the bride.

To make your own sachet mixture, try scented geraniums, powdered cloves, lavender or rose petals. Potpourri also works nicely and may be purchased at craft shops and the perfume counters of many department stores. Or follow the the recipes on the previous page for directions if you'd like to make your own.

3" length of 5"-wide lace, preferably a type with the same design at either edge
3 by 5" piece lining fabric, soft yet closely woven; tulle, organza or fine percale work well
26 to 30" length of woven-edge ribbon, ⅛ to ¼" wide (length should be just enough to go over your head when the ends are joined)
Sachet mixture

1. Turn down each short edge of lining ½ inch to make hems. Press. Center lining on wrong side of lace, with hem edges up. Cross ends of ribbon and place ribbon in center of one hem edge. Stitch to tack down.

2. Fold lace and lining in half, lace sides together. Stitch each side, using ¼-inch seams, leaving top (hemmed) side open. Turn right side out.

3. Fill with sachet mixture. With gathering stitch, hand sew the top together and gather tightly. Be sure gathering stitches are below top of lining so that sachet does not spill. Wind thread two or three times around sachet and fasten.

Sachet Sense

❤ Tuck a secret sachet in a greeting card or letter.

❤ Put one in a lingerie drawer.

❤ Wear one for "slumber jewelry."

❤ Give one to a little girl to wear as scented "play" jewelry.

❤ Make them as favors for a wedding shower.

❤ Give one to an elderly friend to remind her of pleasant, maybe romantic, memories.

My Dear Granddaughter,
I would like you to
have these fragrant beads
of roses to wear next to
your skin under your
gown on your wedding day

Old-time Bridal Beads

My grandmother made the beads for my wedding day, and they still retain their fragrance. It is a comfort to me to keep them in the family. Your grandfather restrung them so you needn't worry that they will break. He added some blue lace agate and marcasite beads from a broken necklace I had been fond of.

Grandmother originally strung the rose beads simply on black button thread without ornaments of any kind. That was her way. Since I had a midsummer wedding too, as you have planned, my grandmother made these from the bright purple and pink ramblers that climbed all over the fence along the side of her house. It's been nice to be reminded still of those fragrant midsummer friends.

It is difficult to believe that the elusive natural fragrance of flowers can be preserved for a century without fading. The warmth of your skin brings it out even more. If you pass this necklace down to your daughter for her wedding day you may want to make a new set for yourself. I have enclosed the method Grandmother told me. She always said the most fragrant roses grow wild along stone walls and fences and around old cellar holes.

When you store the beads, be sure to put a note with them so anyone finding them will know their age and what they are. I've noticed that children are too busy becoming adults to be concerned with traditions, but as they grow older, they become more interested in what has been passed down to them.

With all my love,
Gramma

Recipe for Rose Beads

- Pick the **rose petals** only, or gather fresh ones that have fallen. The petals may be faded but must be fresh, not dried or brown. Gather about a shopping bag full. By picking only the petals, you don't interfere with the bush's ability to produce rose hips later.

- You can grind the petals to a paste with a mortar and pestle, but it is easier to put them through **a hand food grinder**. The result will be a mass that resembles modeling clay, and your kitchen will smell of roses. Put ground petals in **a cast-iron skillet or pot** (be sure there's no rust in the pot), and regrind petals each day for 2 weeks.

- You will see the paste become thicker each day until it reaches a consistency where it can be formed into smooth, hard beads. To do this, roll little lumps (smaller than marbles) between your hands with a circular motion until they are smooth and well rounded. Put a **large common pin** through the center of each and stick the pin into **a soft board**. Continue rolling, piercing and attaching to the board (at least ½ inch apart) until you have as many beads as you need. A dried bead will be half the size of the freshly made one. It will take about 60 beads for an adult-size necklace.

- Let the beads dry for at least 2 weeks, longer if the weather is humid. Remove the pins. String them on **button thread**, using a dark color to blend with the mahogany tones of the beads. With **flannel or other soft cloth**, polish the entire string of beads. (This highlights them and is easier than polishing each bead.) As you wear them, they will darken and polish. If the strand is long enough to slip over your head, you won't need **a clasp**. Otherwise take one off an old necklace or buy one from a jeweler.

T hese are so easy to make! You can buy any old applesauce in a jar and a can of cinnamon. Use our patterns or some tin cookie cutters from the back of a drawer somewhere. That's about it. Next

Spicy Trims

step . . . fragrant gifts that last for years. The ones we made (with expert help from a seven-year-old) are suspended by ⅛-inch satin ribbon bows from the teeth of an old-fashioned farm rake in miniature.

A warm-hearted project for a crisp autumn evening. Perhaps the air in the kitchen is still fragrantly moist from making applesauce that had just a flick of cinnamon in it. And a whisper of clove still hangs in the air.

Nose nose nose nose!
And who gave me this jolly red nose?
Nutmegs and ginger, cinnamon and
*   cloves,*
And they gave me this jolly red nose.
               Thomas Ravenscroft, 1592-1635

6 tablespoons applesauce
9 tablespoons plus 2 teaspoons ground
   cinnamon
1 teaspoon ground cloves
Extra cinnamon for rolling dough
Pastry cloth and rolling pin; small sharp
   knife; small skewer (or other sharp,
   pointed tool); small spatula; cookie
   sheet
Ribbons in variety of colors, 1/16 or 1/8"
   wide; quick-drying craft glue; small
   dried flowers (optional)

1. In a small bowl, combine applesauce, cinnamon and cloves. Stir until well blended, then work with your hands until mix has a smooth, claylike consistency.

2. Generously "flour" pastry cloth and rolling pin with cinnamon. Roll out dough to about 1/8-inch thickness.

3. Using the patterns provided on the pattern sheet, lay pattern pieces directly onto the dough. Cut around the shapes with a small sharp knife. Be sure to cut through entire shape so it can be easily lifted from remaining dough.

4. With a small skewer, mark details on cutout shape; make holes where ribbons will be threaded through for hanging (make holes large enough to thread a ribbon through, but not so large as to weaken the shape).

5. Lift shapes using a small spatula and move them to a cookie sheet.

6. After shapes are cut from rolled dough, gather scraps, re-roll dough and continue cutting out shapes until all dough is used up.

7. Heat oven to 120F and place cookie sheet in oven. After about 1½ hours, turn heat off. Leave cinnamon cutouts in oven 5 to 6 hours or overnight.

8. Tie ribbons onto shapes or thread ribbons through holes in shapes for hanging. Glue ribbon in place, when necessary, for stability. Glue dried flowers in place where desired. Store dried cutouts in an airtight container, layered in tissue or paper towels. Makes about twenty 2-inch shapes.

Idea Bank

• Young children love to help make these and they can.

Verily great grace may go
with a little gift;
and precious are all things
that come from friends.
               Theocritus, c. 310-250 B.C.

• Hang one over a stove because heat helps disperse the fragrance. Or tie some onto a grapevine wreath or a Christmas tree to add a dimension of fragrance to holiday decorations.

• Tuck one between the folds of an embroidered hankie for a bride.

• Tie a Spicy Trim into a bow on a gift-wrapped package.

Virtue is like precious odors—most fragrant when they are incensed or crushed.—Francis Bacon, 1561-1626

• Save tins with tops. Buy real cotton dish towels on sale. Fold the towel to fit into the tin, then pack it by folding it back and forth, accordion style. Lay a Spicy Trim or two in each fold. It will protect them (and make a super-scented kitchen towel gift as well). Seal the lid on with tape around it and put the laden tins aside to have gifts at-the-ready.

As aromatic plants bestow
No spicy fragrance while they grow;
But crushed or trodden to the ground,
Diffuse their balmy sweets around.
               Oliver Goldsmith, 1764

• Write one of the foregoing quotations, as appropriate, on the gift card you enclose with a present of Spicy Trims.

For the Bath

Add the scent of herbs or flowers to a long relaxing bath and you will be sharing a luxury that privileged people have enjoyed since the times of Cleopatra, and even earlier. There are herbs, flowers and scents for every bath-time need: Some simply smell good; others are relaxing, invigorating, soothing, comforting or refreshing.

Although you can make little "tea bags" of herbs to float in your bath water, it is easier to infuse these scents through bath oils and salts that are quite easy to make and have benefits for your skin. To make bath oils and salts, we use fragrant oils which are pressed and distilled from fresh leaves and blossoms. Called essential oils, they are highly concentrated—a bushel of rose petals makes only a tiny vial of oil—so you need very little.

Although perfume oils and those labeled "potpourri oil" are less expensive, they are artificial scents or natural oils cut with cheaper oils or alcohol, and their scents will dissipate quickly. Since so little is needed, and it will be on your skin, it is best to check the labels and use essential oils.

For the recipes that follow, you can use any essential oil whose fragrance pleases you. Rose and lavender are the most popular—rose for a relaxing bath and to soften the skin, lavender for an invigorating bath.

Use chamomile for a relaxing, comforting bath and rosemary to relieve tired muscles. Gardenia, hyacinth, carnation and lily of the valley are all attractive floral scents. Jasmine is a headier floral with oriental overtones. The scent of lavender is crisp and clean, and its very name comes from the Latin word "to wash." Enjoy your pretty and fragrant collection of bath salts and oils or give them as gifts.

Bath Salts

Epsom salts
Essential oils
Liquid food coloring
Clean, dry, wide-mouth jars
  (peanut-butter jars work well)
Soup spoon
Small, fancy jars (we like
  old-fashioned apothecary-
  style)
Jar labels
Narrow satin ribbons

1. Divide salts among several wide-mouth jars, one for each different oil you will be using, filling each jar no more than half full.

2. Add a few drops essential oil to each, labeling so you can tell them apart. Add a tiny drop of food coloring—red for rose, green for rosemary, yellow for chamomile and a touch each of red and blue for lavender.

3. Mix these into the salts, stirring thoroughly and pressing any lumps against side of jar with back of spoon. When the color is evenly distributed, the oil will be, too.

4. Spoon salts into fancy jars and label each. Tie with satin bows, adding little tags if these are to be gifts. Tags should read "Bath Salts; sprinkle 1 teaspoonful over bath water."

Bath Oils

Although bath oils may be made from a "dispersing oil" that mixes with water and distributes itself evenly throughout the bath, the only base oil for these, a treated castor oil, is very hard to obtain. Most commercial bath oils simply spread in a very thin layer over the surface of the water and coat the skin as you enter the tub. Those are easily made from safflower, peanut, sesame, sunflower, avocado or sweet almond oil, or a combination of these, with essential oils added for fragrance.

Use the following recipes or create your own, with the oils listed above and the essential oils recommended for Bath Salts. These recipes make ½ pint of oil, but you may want to make smaller quantities to sample a variety.

Directions for each are simple: Shake the ingredients together to blend well. If Bath Oils are for gifts, package them in small fancy bottles with tight lids, such as those used for salad dressings and fancy vinegars, and dress them up with ribbons as for Bath Salts. Tags should read "Bath Oil; use 1 teaspoonful in a tub of warm water."

English Bath Oil

½ cup safflower oil
½ cup sunflower oil
¼ oz lavender oil

Hungarian Bath Oil

½ cup sesame oil
½ cup safflower oil
⅛ oz rosemary oil
⅛ oz rose oil

Oriental Bath Oil

½ cup peanut oil
¼ cup sesame oil
¼ cup sweet almond oil
½ oz jasmine oil

Tuzzy-Muzzies, Nosegays and Favors

*J*ust yesterday our Victorian Aunt Emily came to mind. A small group of us had gotten together around the dining room table to make up some fabric blooms as party favors. Somehow all the work goes faster with a little tea and a little gossip. How many stitches flew into a quilt on the wings of a good story?

At the very same table one evening years ago, before all of us children were sent off to bed, Aunt Emily told us about Jonathan. Even years later we remembered "The Tale of the Tuzzy-Muzzy."

It happened the summer her parents took Emily with them when they sailed for Europe. They arrived at the pier only to find the sailing had been delayed 3 hours.

To pass the time Emily read her book. Someone began to play the flute. A young man named Jonathan began to dance.

HEAD AND HEELS.

At the time none of the other passengers realized the dance they'd all enjoyed was a dance for Emily. In those days there was no easy way for Jonathan to attract her attention and speaking directly to her was out of the question. But already, he would confess later, he was head and heels over the girl whose name he didn't even know.

The ship would soon sail. At the very last moment he dashed ashore and purchased a small nosegay, or tuzzy-muzzy as they were called at the time, from the pier vendor. And occasionally during the voyage Emily silently favored the boy by carrying the favor he had presented to her on the pier.

Nosegays called tuzzy-muzzies (or tussie-mussies) were popular in colonial times and were often given as gifts to people making a journey. Different flowers and herbs symbolized different things: rosemary and forget-me-nots for remembrance; violets for loyalty; marigolds for happiness, for example.

Make a tuzzy-muzzy of fresh or dried herbs or flowers. Soak a length of pretty grosgrain ribbon in perfume before tying it around the flowers or herbs. The ribbon will dry and the fragrance will last for years.

Show your guests you've gone overboard to make their visit a pleasure with your own fabric flower creations. See page 63 for directions to make fabric blooms and you'll be ready to shower friends with floral hospitality.

A small piece of white or green wire left over from your flower construction could also fasten matching flowers to the candle holders and the napkin rings on your table, creating a lovely floral theme in any colors you choose.

What a charming way to favor your favorite friends and family members at a wedding or baby shower, a ladies' luncheon or an afternoon tea.

Fasten the stem end of one or two flowers to a small comb to be tucked into a young lady's hair, a fashion idea as fresh as it was in Cousin Emily's day.

A traditional way to show your guests that you meant it when you requested "the favor of their presence" is to make a flower favor for each place setting. Place a handful of Jordan almonds, mints or other sweet in an 8-inch square of nylon netting and secure the netting and the stem of a flower with a piece of satin ribbon.

For the most spectacular Christmas ever, gather together all your friends 'round the table in autumn. Make enough blooms to decorate your tree with small fabric flowers nestling in several tuzzy-muzzies, or cover the tree with a snowfall of single flowers.

If the festivities call for a gift, it might look fetching if you slipped a bloom or two through the ribbons on the package.

Certainly, "favoring" your favorite people will take some time, some work and some tea, but just think of the stories and Jonathan's joy at seeing that Emily was carrying his flower favor when she entered the grand dining room on their first night at sea.

O ne of the most important and enjoyable tasks in quilt making is choosing clever combinations of fabrics in different hues and densities to give the project your special touch. These flowers

Fabric Florals

offer the same opportunity and provide the same fun. Browse through the colorful scraps you have on hand and you'll create a garden of lasting blooms with a million uses and with no sewing.

Two or three of these fabric beauties stay fresh as daisies in a bud vase on a desk, adding color without clutter to a work area. Create a colorful patchwork look by making each petal from a different fabric, or use softer combinations for a more formal look.

⅛ yard each of several soft fabrics, including green for leaves (we used pastel calicos and white silk for petals)
Cookie sheet
White and green covered wire (a thin wire covered with fabric, sold in both lengths and spools and in various colors)
2 straight-sided, round bottles with no lip at bottom: 1 about 1" diameter, 1 about ½" diameter (empty medicine bottles work well)
Fabric or white glue
Floral tape
Small dried flowers for stamens
Scissors; florist's foam for arranging

Making the Petals

1. Place the fabric right side up on the cookie sheet.

2. Take a 10-inch length of white wire and wrap it around the larger bottle so that both ends are even. Twist both ends tightly against the bottle to form a petal loop around the bottle. Push the twisted ends up against the bottle until they are at right angles to the loop.

3. Slide the wire loop off the bottle form, taking care the loop remains flat and even. Gently pull the loop to make an oval petal. Prepare a batch of loops: For each double flower you need five large petals (constructed with the 1-inch bottle) and five small petals (made with the ½-inch bottle); to make small flowers, use only five small petals.

4. Pour a puddle of glue about 2 inches wide on a protected surface. If you use white glue, you may find it works better after it sits awhile until it thickens.

5. Dip the wire loop into the glue, making sure it is coated. To blot excess glue, lightly press the loop on a piece of scrap paper.

6. Place the glue-coated loop on top of the fabric and apply a slight amount of pressure. The wire should adhere to the fabric at all points.

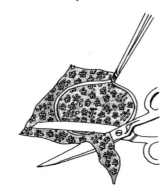

7. After the glue is completely dry, cut around each individual loop. Work carefully when cutting. Cut as close to the wire as possible until no fabric shows on the outside of the petal.

Assembling the Flower

1. Bend the wire ends back straight. Make two stacks of petals: two large and three small petals in one stack and three large and two small petals in the other. All petals should be stacked right side up, with the smaller petals on the top and the stems and loops flat.

2. Place a small bunch of dried flowers on top of one stack of petals. Place the other stack of petals face down on top of the center. Pick up all the petals and the center and, holding them in one hand, wrap the stems with floral tape. Wrap as tightly as possible, stretching the tape as you work. Wrap the rest of the stem by turning the flower with one hand and holding the tape in the other hand.

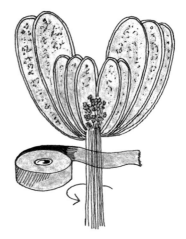

3. Now comes the fun part—arranging the petals. Start with the large outside petals first and pull each one down separately into place. Push up on the edge of each petal until it curves slightly. Then repeat the procedure for each of the small petals.

Making the Leaves

1. Use the ½-inch bottle and green wire; follow the same procedure outlined in steps 1–8 for making petals. After slipping the wire off the bottle, pinch the wire loop slightly with your thumb and forefinger on the side opposite the stem. Make sure the leaf loop stays flat. We used a soft green printed fabric for the leaves and made one or two leaves for each flower.

2. To attach the leaves to the stem, hold the leaf wire ends against the stem and wrap around the stem and leaf wire ends with floral tape. Remember to stretch the tape as you work. Arrange the flowers: Put florist's foam in the bottom of your container to hold the stems and make arranging easier.

Dried Florals

Just as good things are said to come in small packages, miniature floral designs have many uses—package trims, party favors, tree decorations, to name a few.

Wedding Bell

10" piece 2"-wide lace, white or ecru
Sewing thread, color to match lace
Mini silk flowers with wire stems
2½" bell, preferably basket material with attached hanger
Glue gun or craft glue
8" piece metallic thread, gold or silver
Fragrant oil

1. Sew together ends of lace to make a continuous circle. With needle and thread gather top of lace using a running stitch pulled taut.

2. Bunch flowers together. Insert flowers through top of gathered lace and into hanger on bell. Adjust lace and flowers to fit on bell.

3. Using hot glue gun or craft glue, attach silver or gold thread to center of flower bunch.

4. Add a few drops of fragrant oil to flower bunch for floral scent.

Shells make pretty shapes so they are appropriate for a nursery, hung within sight but out of reach. Or try hanging one on the rack holding fresh guest towels in the bath. See page 67 for fragrance suggestions

Summery Straw

⅓ cup potpourri
4½" straw hat
3" circle of netting
Glue gun or craft glue
1 yard ribbon, ¼" wide in desired color
Dried flowers for trim

1. Place potpourri in crown of hat. Cover with netting, gluing the edges down with glue gun or craft glue.

2. Place ribbon around brim and glue together where ends meet. Make a bow with extra ribbon, reserving 3 inches for hanger.

3. Attach dried flowers to bow; glue bow and flowers to hat.

4. Glue 3 inches of ribbon to front inside of brim for a hanger.

When the potpourri needs refreshing, add a few drops of fragrant oil.

Scented Shell

1½ yards of ribbon, ⅜" wide, in one or two color(s) to coordinate with flowers
Small amount of Spanish moss
Sea shell (any shell that appeals to you will work)
Glue gun or strong craft glue
Assorted small dried flowers
Fragrant oil

1. Tie a bow with the ribbon(s), reserving ⅓ yard of ribbon for hanger.

2. Arrange Spanish moss to conform to top of shell and glue into place. Glue bow on top of the moss.

3. Arrange dried flowers on top of bow and moss, then glue into place. Apply fragrant oil to center of flowers.

4. Use ⅓ yard ribbon(s) to make a hanger; glue into place.

Spicy Spoons

Assorted culinary herb seeds: Choose from cardamom, star anise, allspice, poppy, juniper, celery, cloves, fennel, bay leaves, anise and dill (some of these aren't really herbs but they are pretty)
2 wooden spoons, preferably salad or stirring spoons
Glue gun or craft glue
Ribbon
Dried flowers
Wire or eye-screw for a hanger

1. Plan out a pattern of seeds to fit the hollows of the wooden spoons.

2. Apply a small amount of glue to one hollow and place seeds on glue; continue until the area is filled. Repeat for the other spoon. Do small areas at a time—the glue dries quickly.

3. Tie spoons together with ribbon. Place stems of dried flowers beneath ribbon and hold in place with glue.

4. Make a hanger by twisting wire into a small loop. Attach to back of spoons through ribbon.

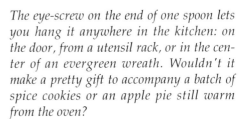

The eye-screw on the end of one spoon lets you hang it anywhere in the kitchen: on the door, from a utensil rack, or in the center of an evergreen wreath. Wouldn't it make a pretty gift to accompany a batch of spice cookies or an apple pie still warm from the oven?

Sweet Annie's Heart

7" wire heart
Various artemisias are
available from an herbary
or florist who handles
dried flowers
1½ yards ribbon, ⅜" wide
Dried flowers
Fine-gauge floral wire
Glue gun or strong craft glue

Artemisia has its own fragrance, so no other scented oils need be added. Its natural fragrance helps to mask other odors such as mildew. Try scattering it around a cat box, hanging it in a kitchen or in smokey areas.

1. Cover wire heart completely with artemisia by bunching and wrapping with fine floral wire. Don't let the artemisia get too wide; glue may help keep it bunched. Allow artemisia to dry completely. (The amount of time this takes depends on the humidity.)

2. Remove floral wire if it shows. Make a double bow using two pieces of ribbon at once; attach bow and dried flowers with glue gun or craft glue. Make a hanger from ribbon if you want it to show or fine floral wire if you want to hide it.

"Sweet Annie" is one common name for Artemisia annua. Use fresh if you can find any. The dried is brittle and more difficult to work with. To renew the fragrance, crush four or five of the berries. As the artemisia dries it will begin to shed. Take the wreath down, tap it gently on a flat surface and hang it back up.

Eucalyptus Crown

These are sturdy and long-lasting, especially if the eucalyptus has been treated with glycerin when you buy it.

Eucalyptus: enough for an 8"
wreath in desired color (green,
blue, red or brown)—1 bunch
is usually enough
Medium-gauge floral wire
1 yard ribbon, ⅜" wide
Glue gun or craft glue
Dried flowers

1. Bend the stalks of eucalyptus to form a ring about 8 inches in diameter, wrapping medium-gauge floral wire beneath the leaves to hold the stalks together (the wire is not removed). Use as many or as few stalks as you wish to get the desired fullness.

The pungent, medicinal odor of eucalyptus is appropriate for a bath. Its oils have been extracted for medicine, but its leaves are poisonous to all animals save one; the koala bears of Australia live on them.

2. Wrap ribbon around wreath as shown, ending with a bow at the top tied prettily. If necessary, glue beneath the bow to hold it in position.

3. Attach dried flowers with stems showing beneath bow; glue them in place behind the bow.

4. Make a hanger by twisting floral wire into a dime-sized circle. Attach to wire used to form the wreath or to a eucalyptus stem.

Herbal Favors

Fragrance can be as delightful an accent as the colors, lighting and textures that make each room in your home pretty and pleasant. Make it part of your table decor so a simple buffet becomes memorable. Above, keeping fragrant company with the charming antique Quimper pottery of Brittany are the fresh herbs of Provence: (clockwise from top left) thyme, sage, rosemary, tarragon, winter savory and basil. Their natural fragrance will complement any simple dish prepared with herbs, as fragrant flowers might.

Your sense of smell evokes memories from your past. When a guest or family member smells the scent of orange, he or she will perhaps remember seeing Grandma warming the peels on the woodstove or mother squeezing fresh orange juice. You'll also be creating new scent-inspired memories for family and friends. Often, as a family gathers for Sunday dinner, the members are greeted with the aroma of herb-stuffed chicken roasting in the oven. Later, when one smells herbs growing in the garden, she is pleasantly reminded of dinner at Grandma's house.

Roasted Herbed Chicken

2½ to 3-lb chicken
Salt
Freshly ground pepper
Assorted fresh herbs to taste (rosemary, tarragon, thyme, sage, parsley, basil or oregano)
1 small onion, peeled
Olive oil

1. Preheat oven to 350F. Wash and dry chicken inside and out. Remove any excess fat. Salt inside of chicken.
2. Cut 2- to 3-inch spears of herbs to be used and wash if necessary.
3. Stuff herbs into chicken cavity along with onion.
4. Place chicken in a small roasting pan. Brush with olive oil.
5. Roast uncovered for about 1 hour. When leg moves easily or no pink liquid seeps from breast when pierced with fork, chicken is done. Serve hot or cold. Makes 4 servings.

Pantry Pest Preventers

Most herbs work well in the pantry, but there are a few that will also help keep away pesky food moths as well as provide pleasant fragrance. Combine scent with function by hanging sage, wormwood, lavender and lemongrass. The moths are repelled naturally—no need to use chemicals around your foodstuffs.

In the Kitchen

Fresh herbs in pots will be both useful and fragrant in the kitchen, where herbs from the garden are traditionally washed, tied and hung to dry. Drying herbs adds to the charm of the decor and their fragrance creates a pleasant kitchen memory.

Cinnamon sticks are both decorative and scented. They can be tied with bows with the colors of the season and hung on the wall or placed in a basket. Combine with other spices to decorate a pretty kitchen utensil like the spoon on page 64. Dried citrus peels, cloves, nutmeg, star anise, sassafras root and allspice work well. Try filling an old-fashioned soap shaker with a fragrant mix or simmering a mix of orange rind, whole cloves and cinnamon in cider or water.

Sweet basil

For the Bath

Dried lavender, roses, chamomile and orange flowers can be tied up in cotton sachets and stacked in little baskets with colorful, scented soaps on the counter of your bathroom. Just toss a sachet into the running bath water and later use it to rub the scented water on your skin. Children are especially pleased if you use citrus peels and hibiscus flower. They leave the bath water a delightful pink color but won't hurt sensitive skin. Pungent, masking fragrances such as eucalyptus and clove are appropriate in a lavatory, too.

Lavender and Linens

Remember your grandmother's linen closet smelling like lavender? It also serves as a moth repellent. Some think that lavender also induces sleep, so storing it among your linens may help your household float off to dreamland more easily. Lavender and other concentrated oils are available at herb, and some craft, shops.

Sweet Dreams

The bedroom invites floral scents like roses, violets, sweet pea, peach and apple blossoms or lily of the valley.

Floral scents have a calming effect, so decorative sleep pillows filled with linden flowers, hops, chamomile flowers and cloves make wonderful accents for the bed and are soothing for both adults and children on those occasional sleepless nights.

Fragrant Celebrations

Create happy "scent memories" by using a single scent throughout your house for a particular holiday or celebration:

Simmer on the stove top:

 Apple peels and nutmeg for a whiff of the first day of autumn

 Cinnamon and cloves at Halloween

Use fresh cuttings or essential oils of:

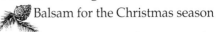 Balsam for the Christmas season

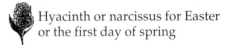 Hyacinth or narcissus for Easter or the first day of spring

Everyone has a favorite scent. For a family member's birthday, fill the house with that scent to create a very personal fragrant celebration. A variety of fragrant oils can be found in craft and specialty shops to apply to any pretty craft project or gift.

Fresh Herb Pad

The fragrance of bubbling casseroles or steaming teapots adds cozy warmth to any dining or tea-sipping occasion. Who can resist the aroma of cloves with ham or orange spice with tea? Enhance those wonderful fragrances and protect your table at the same time with this easy-to-make hot pad. Tuck fresh herbs to complement your meal inside the triangular pockets of the quilted pad. The heat from the container you set on it will release the herbs' fragrance into the air. Since only basic cutting, folding and sewing skills are required, this is a perfect project for someone who is learning to sew.

Making these pieced and quilted pockets follows many of the cutting, assembling and stitching techniques used in making the squares for a quilt. These useful and decorative pads can easily be made in batches to sell at fundraisers or to give at holiday time (when there are lots of hot dishes and beverages around the house). If you make one for your own dining table, choose fabrics that match your place mats or napkins. For parties, make several that will coordinate with your dining room decor, then serve dishes buffet-style with their matching pads. The materials listed allow enough fabric to make 10 pads.

½ yard of 45" quilted polyester batting faced with fabric of coordinating color (or use denim or corduroy) for bottom
1 yard of 45" lightweight print fabric (A)
1 yard of 45" lightweight fabric in coordinating color or print (B)
Thread to match fabrics
Ruler; soft pencil or chalk
Fresh or dried herbs and spices

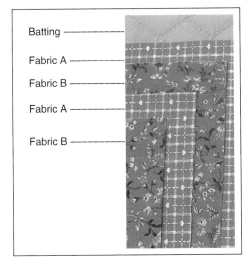

1. Cut a 9-inch square from the batting fabric. This will pad the bottom with its fabric side showing. Cut two 9-inch squares from each of the lightweight fabrics (**A** and **B**), for the hot-pad top. With right side facing, fold each fabric square diagonally to form four triangles, two of fabric **A** and two of fabric **B**. Press each triangle to form a crease on the fold.

2. Place the batting right side up on a flat surface. Place the triangles of fabric on it, wrong side up, as follows: Align the 9-inch-long raw edges of one fabric **A** triangle with the top and right edges of the batting. Add and overlap one fabric **B** triangle, aligning the 9-inch-long raw edges of that triangle with the right and bottom edges of the batting.

3. Add and overlap the second fabric **A** triangle, aligning the 9-inch-long raw edges with the bottom edge and left side of the batting. Add the second fabric **B** triangle, aligning the 9-inch-long raw edges with the left and top edges of the batting. Overlap the lower fabric **A** triangle; tuck the fabric **B** triangle under the top fabric **A** triangle. Adjust center points of triangles to overlap neatly. Pin through all layers.

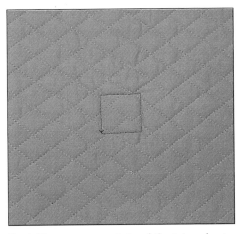

4. Leaving a ½-inch seam allowance, machine-stitch all edges through all layers. Trim seams to ⅛ inch. Turn the pad right side out. Adjust corners by pushing out with the eraser end of the pencil.

5. Adjust center points of the triangles to meet evenly. With a soft pencil, mark a 1-inch square around each point at the center. Machine-stitch through to the back, as shown, to anchor the fabric.

You can use either dried or fresh herbs and spices to stuff the pockets of your hot pad. Select one or a combination of items that will complement the taste and fragrance of the dish or dishes you bring to the table. For example, use cinnamon and cloves when serving hot apple pie; try sage and tarragon with a chicken casserole; use mint or rosemary with lamb; either thyme or lemon balm with fish. When you tuck sprigs of fresh herbs into the pockets, leave a little peeking out for decoration. After the meal, don't forget to shake out the contents before washing or storing the pad.

Fresh Herb Pad   69

Silk Floral Arrangements

Each spring the Museum of Fine Arts, Boston, invites floral arrangers into the museum to interpret selected paintings, sculptures and artifacts with their own fresh-flower artistry. The museum originated this exciting exhibit concept and called it *Art in Bloom*. Betty Brown, an exhibit organizer and floral artist who lectures nationally on *Art in Bloom*, shares her knowledge here.

Creating a flower arrangement to complement a work of art is challenging and rewarding. You don't need original art or fresh flowers to create an art-in-bloom addition to your decor. We chose silk flowers to complement this framed poster of "Mother and Child in a Boat," a painting by Edmund C. Tarbell from the collection of the Museum of Fine Arts, Boston.

You don't have to be an artist to have fun arranging flowers. Just let a work of art inspire you. Your flower arrangement should capture the mood of the subject or art period in color, texture and composition. For example, Tarbell, an American portrait and genre painter, was a founding father of the "Ten American Painters," admirers of French Impressionism. He enjoyed portraying women out of doors in genteel tradition. "Mother and Child in a Boat" (1892) captures a tender, tranquil, sun-dappled scene. The subjects and the colors—the young woman's soft pink dress, her child's white dress and blue shoes, the cream-colored rowboat and the green of leaves reflected on the blue water—all contribute to the visual and emotional impact of the painting.

Our silk flower arrangement is designed to mirror the serenity of the mother and child at leisure. A casual basket is filled with an exquisite grouping of delicate spring flowers, which complement the colors and textures in the art masterpiece.

Blue delphinium are used for the main lines of the design. These stems are placed to define the height and the width of the design, and to lead your eye toward the painting. (Notice how the arrangement gently wraps around the print.) White peonies and pink roses are the focal point of the arrangement and repeat the pink and white in the mother's and child's clothing. Other flowers used include lavender lilac, blue sweet peas, pink bolsamina, hot-pink flowering sumac, white iris and lavender anemones with dark centers. Ferns, huckleberry foliage and green moss, which covers the floral foam base, complete the arrangement. See page 45 for basic arranging tips.

Artwork of your choice: painting, sculpture or decorative art
Silk flowers and green foliages
Container for flower arrangement
Wire cutters, for cutting flower stems
Mechanics (supports for your flowers): dry, brown floral foam, sold in blocks, to hold stems in place; sticky floral clay; anchor pins; green floral tape; floral wire (straight, not spool wire), to lengthen stems; green moss or gray Spanish moss, to conceal foam in completed design

Delphinium establish height and width of arrangement and draw viewer's eye to painting.

Focal point

Focal point of arrangement.

Smaller secondary flowers add fullness.

Select flowers with colors, shapes and textures that are appropriate for your artwork. Scale is important, too: dainty flowers for a small work of art, larger flowers for a larger work of art. Your container should be suitable in shape, style and size for the setting in which the arrangement and artwork will be placed, formal or informal. Try good quality baskets, ceramic and metal containers. Don't scrimp on anchoring and support material. Your arrangement must be very stable so it won't fall apart. Always set up your work area with your artwork in place as it will be displayed. Stand back often as you go along, to see how your container and arrangement are working with your painting or art object.

1. Cut floral foam to fit container, wedging it into place firmly. Or, if your container is low and flat, you can secure the foam by putting a piece of floral clay on the bottom of each anchor pin, then press down onto the dry, clean, dust-free container. Impale the foam onto the upturned prongs of the anchor pins. This base must be secure before you proceed.

2. The height and width of the design are always the first lines to be placed. Place silk flower stems into the foam, curving and bending wire stems as desired for graceful lines. In our arrangement, the long stems of the blue delphinium define the shape of the design and gently guide the viewer's eye to the painting.

3. The point at which the height and width of the design intersect becomes the focal point of the arrangement. In our arrangement, the point at which the tall flowers (delphinium) meet the shorter, fuller flowers (white peonies and pink roses), close to the basket's rim, is the center of interest.

4. Use wire cutters to shorten stems to correct length. To lengthen stems, tape on extra wire with floral tape. If a heavy stem swivels in place, add a second parallel wire stem with floral tape, then insert into floral foam.

5. Place smaller, secondary flowers around the center of interest, some set deep into the arrangement to cover the base, others set toward the outside, to give an airy feel to the design. We used lavender, lilac, blue sweet peas, pink bolsamina, flowering sumac, white iris and lavender anemones as secondary flowers in our arrangement.

6. When all the flowers are in place, complete the design by adding greens and covering foam with moss.

"Mother and Child in a Boat" and other posters may be ordered by writing to: Museum of Fine Arts, Catalog Sales, P.O. Box 1044, Boston, MA 02120.

Baskets with Bows

Hurray for baskets! These pretty catchalls are both decorative and functional. Put your knitting or needlework in a basket. Use one for wastepaper next to a desk. Keep one on a coffee table to hold cocktail napkins, a small plant or coasters. Place one on a bureau or vanity to hold cosmetics. Use one in a child's room for a hamper. Fill one with kitchen gadgets or baby necessities for a shower gift. The possibilities are endless. Inexpensive purchased baskets, either natural or painted white, are waiting for you to beautify them. Your baskets will become the focal point of a room with a few easy-to-learn techniques that make all the difference.

Basket Bows

Fabric, enough to make bow
Fabric stiffener (available in craft stores)
Wax paper; floral wire; glue gun or tacky glue

Just adding a bow can transform a plain-Jane basket into a smashing beauty. The most important consideration here is choosing terrific fabric and making sure the bow is the right size for the basket. If you've found a big basket like the one above, don't be afraid to make a fabulously large bow. A smaller basket obviously calls for a smaller bow, but not too small—it should be a real decorative standout. Choose fabric that will complement the decor. Use drapery fabric remnants or a wallpaper companion fabric.

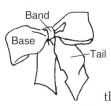

Make your bow in three pieces: the base, the band and the tail. The base and tail should be the same width, but the length of the tail is up to you.

Pour fabric stiffener into a shallow dish and dilute with an equal amount of water. Mix thoroughly. Saturate the bow base with stiffener–water mixture and squeeze out excess liquid. Place the fabric on wax paper or other non-

absorbent surface. Fold top and bottom in at center of base so they overlap. Bring ends together at this center point so that they also overlap. Pinch center

together and secure with a length of floral wire cut long enough also to wrap around bow band and basket handle later. Saturate band next, squeeze out excess and fold edges on long sides under. Wrap around center of bow base, overlapping in the back, and secure to basket handle with wire. Saturate the bow's tail as before, then squeeze excess liquid out and drape between the basket handle and bow so that tails are equal length. Fold ends of tail under at an angle; let dry.

If your basket doesn't have a handle, you can make your bow with two pieces: a base and one piece to form the band and tail. The process is the same until you attach the band. Wrap the band around the base, twist fabric together at the back and arrange tails with ends folded up on an angle. Lay the bow carefully on wax paper and let dry. When the bow is stiff, glue it to the basket with a glue gun or tacky glue.

You can add subtle color to a white basket by applying a wash to the surface. Use any color acrylic paint. Dip a dense sponge into the paint, blot excess paint off onto a nonabsorbent surface like tinfoil and wash the basket with the sponge. Let dry.

Fantastic Florals

Flowers *on* baskets will cultivate the same rave reviews that accompany flowers arranged *in* baskets. Flowers can look especially appropriate and eye-catching on an open-weave, natural-looking basket like the one above. To complement that natural look, simply arrange **silk flowers and ivy** in a graceful arc following the lines of the basket and handle, secure your arrangement with **floral wire** and attach it to your basket with a **glue gun or tacky glue**.

To make a more dressed-up statement, add a bow made of **paper ribbon** (purchased at a craft supply store). Arrange a small bouquet of silk flowers, taking into consideration the shape and size of your basket, and secure your arrangement with floral wire. Make a bow with as many loops as you like and a tail that is in proportion with the basket and flowers. Attach the bow to the flowers with floral wire, then attach the entire arrangement to the basket with a **glue gun** or **tacky glue**.

Dried flowers add a feminine touch to symmetrical, tightly woven baskets like the one shown below. Arrange the bouquet and secure it with floral wire. If the basket has open areas as part of its weaving pattern, take advantage and weave **wide ribbon** around the basket, then tie a bow around the bouquet. If you can't weave through the basket, tie the ribbon around the flowers and glue onto the basket with a **glue gun** or **tacky glue.**

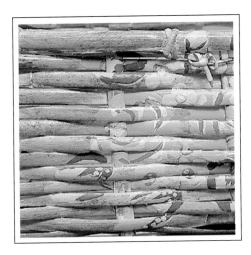

Painted Baskets

Since baskets have such bumpy surfaces, it's hard to paint painstakingly detailed motifs on them. That can be a plus if you just want to create splashes of color, as with the simple floral motif on the basket above. There's no need for great painting skills—the simpler the design the better. Practice sketching on paper. Adapt a flower or other motif from your wallpaper or upholstery, or a geometric design from a quilt. Once you're happy with the design and have experimented with colors, hand paint your motif on the basket. One well-placed motif looks nice, or repeat the motif around the outside or inside of your basket. All you need to hand paint your basket are **acrylic paints**, an assortment of **different-sized brushes** and a basket!

Fabric Motifs

Hand painting isn't for everyone. If you would rather add color without the risk of a slip of the brush, try applying a cutout motif from **chintz fabric**, like the pretty floral spray above, right. Again, you may want to choose a motif that matches your decor, or look through remnants at a decorator-fabric store. One large eye-catching motif looks better than lots of little cutouts, so think bold. The magic ingredient for this process is **Mod Podge**, a gloss-luster water-base combination glue and seal-

er. Cut out your fabric motif with sharp scissors and place it print-side down on tinfoil. Using a no. 10 paintbrush, paint the fabric with Mod Podge, making sure to cover the edges. Place the motif on the basket, pressing into the basket weave with your finger. Let dry. Add a second coat of Mod Podge to give the motif a glossy finish.

Paper Magic

The basket to the right has a secret. What looks like a sophisticated rice-paper finish is really a layer of **paper napkins**. Look in any party and paper supply store and you'll see that paper napkins have beautiful, in some cases museum-inspired, patterns on them. Choose a package of pretty napkins with an all-over design. If the napkins have plain borders, cut them off. Then simply place the napkins on the basket and paint with **Mod Podge**, overlapping napkins just a bit. Let dry. A second coat of Mod Podge will give your basket a glossy finish.

Cut-and-Pierced Lamp Shades

A floral pattern from your wallpaper or upholstery fabric, a design from your carpet or the motif from a favorite quilt can provide the inspiration for a lamp shade. If you have a favorite lamp with a not-so-favorite shade, you can carefully take the lamp shade apart, save the rings and trace the shade to make a pattern for a new shade. Lamp shade paper comes in assorted colors or add color by painting your design with watercolors, as described on page 79.

Warmth and elegance are the keynotes of cut-and-pierced lamp shades. No one is sure where or when the first of these shades was made, but one Connecticut crafter who has been making them for 50 years speculates that they were originally inspired by early pierced-tin lanterns. Fruit and flower motifs, like those shown above, are traditional favorites. Select the one that best complements your decor and use the full-size iron-on patterns we've provided for the shade and four motifs. Cutting and piercing instructions are given below and shade assembly instructions appear on the opposite page.

12 by 30" pieces shade and lining papers (available in craft and lamp parts stores)
Tube water colors, desired colors (optional)
Quality watercolor brushes (optional): 0 for fine work and nos. 1, 2 and 3
Piercing tool, or large needle with eye end pushed into a cork
Craft knife with very sharp no. 11 blades
Piece of glass large enough to work on
Terry cloth towel
Craft glue that dries fast and clear
1 pair shade rings: 6" for top and 10" for bottom
About 35 spring-type clothespins
1½ yards grosgrain ribbon, ⅝" wide, in color to match shade paper
1½ yards velvet ribbon, ¼" wide, in contrasting color
Iron, to transfer designs on bound-in sheet

Examine your lamp before purchasing rings. You may need a clip-on style, a washer-top ring that screws on and is topped by a finial, or a ring that fits on a chimney.

Piercing and Cutting

1. Cut out or photocopy the pattern on the full-size pattern sheet provided. Tape it onto a large piece of folded paper, following pattern marks. Cut around it to make a full pattern. Trace that onto shade paper and cut out. Trace it onto lining paper, adding ½ inch all around. Cut out.

2. Iron motif (see large, bound-in pattern sheet provided) onto the shade paper, centering it carefully. Pass iron lightly for a faint image. Make cuts on this side of the shade.

3. If you plan to paint your shade, now is the time. See the instructions and suggestions in the box opposite.

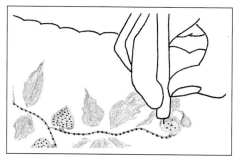

4. Place a folded terry cloth towel between paper and glass and pierce the dots, holding piercing tool or needle perpendicular to the paper. Holes should be no closer than ½ inch apart.

5. With craft knife, cut carefully along lines, working over a sheet of glass. Change blades in knife whenever the edge seems to drag. Be sure to leave all spaces between cuts so design areas remain anchored to the paper.

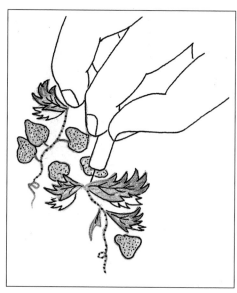

6. Open all cuts slightly by running a needle along them to separate the sides. Very gently, curve petals and leaf tips toward you, molding them into smooth curves with your fingers. Give them plenty of depth, since they will flatten slightly against lining.

When cutting heavy paper or stencils with a craft knife, use only the tip of the blade, holding it firmly and drawing it toward you. With the other hand, guide and turn the paper to make smooth curves. Do not lift the knife from the paper until you have completed each line.

Assembling the Shade

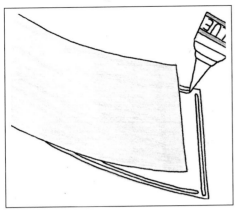

1. Apply very thin lines of glue to straight sides and top (smaller) curved edge of shade. Press the lining in place. Lining should be a bit loose and puffy. The wrinkles won't show and if the lining is too tight the shade will buckle. Apply glue to bottom edge of shade and smooth lining downward, pressing firmly at glued edge. Allow glue to dry.

2. Trim away excess lining paper so it matches shade paper.

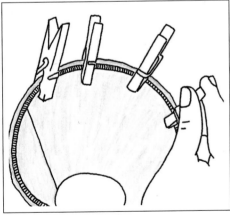

3. Clip long edge of the lined shade paper to the larger (bottom) ring, using the flat sections of spring-type clothespins to grip the ring. Begin at center and work toward straight edges of paper. Hold with a clothespin every 2 to 3 inches, taking care to keep paper evenly pulled between them. Straight edges should overlap slightly. Repeat for top ring by dropping it into the shade. Be sure none of the spokes on top ring is near seam.

4. When both rings are held firmly in place with clothespins, remove one clothespin at a time and carefully apply glue to outside of ring. Clip glued section with clothespin before moving on to the next clothespin. Work from center and be sure paper remains smooth.

5. Apply glue evenly but sparingly to overlapped side seam and press firmly to hold it in place until glue dries. If seam looks like it is beginning to buckle, lay it on its side, seam down, and weight it with a round object (such as a full bottle) until glue dries. If necessary, trim top and bottom flush with rings using sharp scissors.

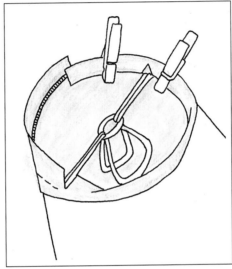

6. Apply a thin line of glue along outside of top edge of shade and cover with grosgrain ribbon, leaving half its width extending over top of shade. Butt ends neatly over seam in shade, but do not overlap ribbon ends. Allow glue to dry, then apply glue inside shade and fold ribbon over top. Press firmly in place over ring, securing with clothespins, if necessary, until dry. If spokes are not recessed, you must clip edge of ribbon with scissors at each spoke to bring ribbon down smoothly. Repeat at bottom edge of shade.

Glue velvet ribbon to lamp shade, just at edge of grosgrain ribbon, without allowing their edges to overlap. Butt ends of velvet ribbon over seam in lamp shade.

Grosgrain ribbon that is part cotton works better than all-nylon ribbon. It has more "give" so it stretches nicely around the shade and glue sticks to it better.

Painting Your Motif

Use artist's watercolors, that come in a tube, diluted to a very watery consistency to paint your shade. A white, ecru or pale pastel paper works best. There are three effective ways to add color to your design.

• If you'd like just a hint of color, use a no. 1 brush and carefully outline your motif.

• For more color with less risk, you can paint on the inside of your shade, adding color to match your decor. The result, when the light is on, will be a lovely, very subtle hint of color. Since you paint before you cut and pierce, you're only risking a piece of shade paper if you end up with an unhappy result.

• If you want the glory of full-blown color, practice first tracing your motif on a piece of plain paper. Once you've got the result you like, recreate it on your shade paper. Remember that when the light is on, your colors will look lighter and more translucent than they do when you're painting on a flat surface.

Theorem Stencil Technique

Theorem, circa 1839, New England. Watercolor on velvet; 17½ by 22½ inches (framed). Artist unknown.

Theorem painting, or stenciling on white velvet, is a 19th-century art. It was popular not only for the beauty of the finished work but because the result could be accomplished by anyone who worked carefully.

The soft effect is quite easy to achieve, and its pale, weathered tones give theorems the appearance of age. While the finished pieces may be made into pillow tops, they are more often framed and hung on the wall.

"Bowl of Fruit," 20th-century theorem. Watercolor on velvet; 14 by 18 inches. Artist unknown.

A favorite design motif for theorem painters has always been a basket or bowl of fruit. By varying shades from dark to light on the deeply textured velvet, the illusion of roundness and depth is easy to achieve, so that an assortment of fruits in different colors shows off the technique at its best. The examples shown here and on the following pages, all from the Museum of American Folk Art, are for inspiration. Instructions for a simplified theorem follow.

The word *theorem* is from the old word for "stencil." Theorems were used for decorating walls, floors, furniture and floorcloths as well as tin trays and boxes. The word, however, survives only in describing stenciling on white velvet.

Unlike other forms of stenciling, theorem does not require a separate stencil for each color. As long as the areas are not contiguous, they can be painted in different colors from the same stencil. This way, two grapes which will be the same color will be on different stencils if they are next to (touching) each other. This basic difference in theorem painting technique allows for a more natural-looking design, without the little "bridges" between colors that are the trademark of many other types of stenciling.

Areas numbered 1 in the diagram on page 82 will be cut on one stencil, areas numbered 2 on a second stencil and areas numbered 3 will be on a third; this design requires only three stencils.

As with any handwork, stencil cutting requires some practice. Before cutting your theorem, practice cutting with your X-Acto knife on some large scraps of waxed stencil paper to get the feel of the knife and the paper.

Waxed stencil paper (sold in craft stores)
Large sheet of glass, masking-taped around all edges, to cut the stencils on
2 pieces heavy cardboard (mat board works well), each the size of the velvet
White glue
Off-white cotton velvet or velveteen, at least 4" larger than the stencil
Transparent oil paints: cadmium red (medium), chrome yellow, Prussian blue, burnt umber and vert emeraude
Small piece of foil (for palette)
5 squares of wool flannel, 4" each (1 for each color)
Small paintbrush (for glue)
Ruler
Soft-lead pencil
X-Acto knife
Masking tape
No. 1 or no. 00 sable artist's paintbrush

1. Using a photocopying machine, enlarge the theorem artwork on page 82 by 150% (or to the size you desire). Trace outlines onto waxed stencil paper, using the numbers in the dia-

"Tray of Fruit," 20th-century theorem. Watercolor on velvet; 15¼ inches by 18⅞ inches. Artist unknown.

gram to guide you in cutting three stencils. Working carefully, cut out each stencil following the pencil lines. Try to make all (or several) cuts in one direction, then turn the stencil and cut in the opposite direction. Cut *slightly* past each intersection so pieces will lift out easily. Set stencils aside.

2. Evenly brush one piece of cardboard or mat board with white glue. Let it stand for a moment until it is tacky, then lay the velvet, face up, on the glued surface and smooth out all wrinkles. Lift and pull edges slightly if necessary to get a perfectly even surface. Allow glue to dry thoroughly.

To avoid staining fabric, brush any stray glue off quickly with a damp cloth. Velvet tends to leave little bits of nap wherever it goes. Be sure none of this lint gets on the back of the velvet or the glued surface of the cardboard or mount. If it does, this slightly raised dot will take up more paint than the surrounding area and become a dark spot on your finished work.

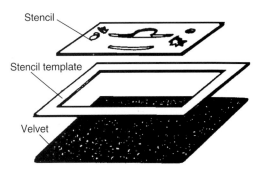

3. Center one of the stencils on the other cardboard piece, measuring so that borders are exactly the same, and draw around it with a pencil. Using the X-Acto knife, cut out this center, forming a frame with outside measurements to match the velvet exactly and inside measurements to match the stencil. By using this frame as a template, you can avoid measuring each time you change your stencil or having to draw guidelines on velvet. The frame will also protect edges from paint smudges.

4. Tape mounted velvet to work surface, then match the frame to its edges and tape that over the velvet.

5. Set first stencil inside frame and secure with tape.

6. Arrange small dabs of paint on foil palette. Put a piece of flannel over your finger and barely touch it to paint on foil. Rub the flannel on a scrap of cloth until most of the paint is off. Working from edge to center of each cutout area of stencil, paint with soft, light strokes. To make an area darker, go over it again, but do not try to hurry the process by using more paint on the flannel.

7. Repeat with other stencils, being careful to keep each successive stencil aligned with frame, until entire picture appears on velvet. Leave a small, unpainted area near center of each rounded piece of fruit to form highlights for roundness and dimension.

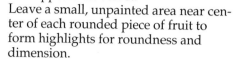

8. Make any necessary corrections freehand with sable brush, darkening veins of leaves and touching up spaces where colors don't meet. Paint tiny yellow seeds on the strawberries freehand.

If you make a little spot of paint on the velvet where it doesn't belong and where another part of the design won't cover it, you can't remove it without ruining the surface of the velvet. But you can often cover it with a tiny addition. A spot beside the design could be covered with an extra leaf, perhaps balanced by another on the other side. A spot beneath the basket could be covered with a single strawberry, as though it had fallen from the basket. Although you might not have chosen to rearrange the design motif thus, it is better than having an obvious mistake marring your finished art.

THEOREM COLOR GUIDE

Paint pear yellow, darker at edges, lighter toward center.

Paint larger section of peach yellow, blushing to orange from center right up to crease. Color line separates sections, as smaller segment is all yellow.

Paint melon yellow first, then paint over with green at edges, leaving centers of each segment yellow.

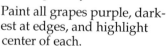
Paint all grapes purple, darkest at edges, and highlight center of each.

Paint cherries red, then paint over edges in a darker red (mix paint with a touch of

burnt umber to darken), leaving centers bright red.

Paint strawberries yellow, shaded with red, darker at edges and tops. Paint basket yellow and shade one side of each strip with yellow mixed with umber.

Paint stems and tendrils brown and leaves green, a little darker at edges.

This theorem, titled "Fruit, Bird and Butterfly," was created by an unknown artist around 1830. A sophisticated example of this craft, the design was worked in watercolor on velvet. Notice how the artist created an almost touchable ripeness by leaving small unpainted areas in the centers of the fruits, then applying darker colors to further enhance the fullness. This process is described on page 82. Before beginning your project, it might be helpful to practice this technique on a small scrap of velvet.

Theorem motifs need not be limited to works on velvet. Use our pattern or cut your own from favorite motifs in wallpaper or fabric, then create theorems using watercolor on paper. Small motifs make lovely designs for note cards.

A cabbage rose dredges up memories from long ago: a pillow from grandmother's damask sofa and the little footstool that graced her dim Victorian parlor; the dining-room chairs from

Classic Cabbage Rose

your great-aunt's home where, for the first time, you sat at the "adult table" on Thanksgiving. Make your own needlepoint memory, following instructions by one of America's foremost needlepoint designers.

Needlepoint is a broad term describing a wide array of needlework styles, all of which are worked on evenly spaced canvas. *Petitpoint* refers to needlepoint worked on 18-gauge or higher canvas; *grospoint* is worked on gauges lower than 18. Gauge refers to canvas size or number of threads per inch—the higher the gauge, the smaller the stitches must be.

Many types of yarns are used for needlepoint: rug yarn, tapestry yarn, Persian yarn, crewel yarn, embroidery floss, pearl cotton, matte embroidery cotton and metallic thread. Best results are achieved when the yarn is coordinated with the canvas gauge. Finer threads or yarns work well for petitpoint while heavier yarns are preferred for grospoint. Persian yarn is used here as it offers excellent coverage of 14-mesh canvas.

This design also lends itself beautifully to cross-stitch. Use 14-count Aida cloth in place of needlepoint canvas and embroidery floss (three strands) instead of Persian yarn.

Covering the canvas evenly and well is the hallmark of quality needlepoint. When beginning a new piece, experiment with yarn types and number of strands to determine what works well. Tension is also important: Stitches worked too tightly allow canvas to show through and distort the shape of the final piece; stitches worked too loosely stand out and are subject to snagging.

18 by 18" canvas, no. 14 mesh
Persian yarn
126 yards black
5 yards pale yellow
5 yards medium yellow
17 yards white
14 yards pale mint
26 yards medium mint
15 yards dark mint
12 yards bright grass green
9 yards pale blue
9 yards medium blue
7 yards dark blue
15 yards light apple green
21 yards medium misty green
10 yards dark blue green
27 yards light shell pink
27 yards medium shell pink
14 yards dark shell pink
24 yards light bright coral
15 yards dark bright coral
12 yards light rose
10 yards medium rose
14 yards bright rose
13 yards dark rose
Masking tape
Waterproof marking pen
Tapestry needle

The chart for this motif can be found on the pattern pages.

Working the Needlepoint

1. Bind all four edges of canvas with masking tape. With marking pen, write "Top" on the top edge. Count canvas threads; mark center of each side and center of canvas using marking pen (the graphite of a pencil may rub off onto yarn).

2. Label each color of yarn by name and symbol used on chart on transfer page.

3. Beginning in center of canvas, work continental stitch with one strand medium shell pink as indicated on chart. Use *two* strands of yarn throughout the rest of the design.

4. Work outward from center in any direction you prefer, following the chart for color and stitch placement. Continue until the floral motif including leaves and bows is completed. Try to complete all the color in one area before changing to a different color, but when this requires too much "skipping around," change colors and go back to the first color later.

To anchor a new yarn, leave a 1- to 2-inch piece free in back of the canvas. Hold yarn against the canvas and catch it in the first several stitches. Snip off excess.

5. Fill in background with black. Surround design with as much black as you desire to achieve the size you want (the needlepoint in the photograph measures 14 by 14 inches).

To prevent canvas from showing through large areas of very dark colors, you may want to paint those areas with black acrylic paint before starting to stitch. However, dark canvas is harder on the eyes and makes center markings harder to see.

Finishing

If your finished work is not perfectly square, it should be blocked before framing or preparing for other uses such as a pillow or footstool. To block, dampen needlework slightly with cold water, then fasten it to a board at each corner and at center of each side with rustproof push-pins or thumbtacks. Continue pinning until you have placed pins no more than ½ inch apart all around the piece. Allow the piece to dry completely.

Furniture designed for needlepoint is available through needlepoint shops.

From the Field & Garden

Something seems so right about arranging herbal plantings in an exotic knot or in a small circle where two walkways cross, and marking the center with a sundial. Perhaps the role herbs have played in ancient medicine and pagan rituals also expresses itself as such patterns in the gardener's mind.

In addition to these two ancient and elegant garden layouts, this chapter contains an alphabetical picture-guide to 39 different herbs and spices which tells how each is best used in cooking and what ancient "grandmother wisdom" tells us of their healing properties. The floral craftsperson can select among two dozen thoughtful gift ideas that are easily made—even in batches for garden shops—from step-by-step instructions that teach handcraft skills centuries old. The gardener may want to turn to pages 90-93 for 10 charming gift ideas from gardeners, a chart on forcing 11 common bulbs, and tips on caring for fresh flowers.

Herb Gardens

In the castle grounds of Tudor England, elaborate plantings often contained a knot-garden situated below a window. In "open" knots, the plantings were defined by grass, stones or colored soil. In "closed" knots, such as the example shown here, the spaces around the knot's pattern were filled with other plantings of a single contrasting color.

Persian-style Knot-Garden

Layout

Begin with a pencil sketch. Next, pierce a hole in the bottom of a tin can and fill it with lime. Lay out your garden design with the lime as you "walk" your pattern across the area you have chosen for your garden. Connect one end of a string to a stake and the other end to a lime-filled tin can. As you walk, the lime will trace a circular pattern.

The purple blossoms visible in the corners of this close-up view of the knot are circle onions. The blue-green strands are blue mound and common rue. The square, dark-green borders are germander.

An overall view of the knot-garden reveals two rectangular beds that flank two sides. Junipers add height so visitors will not step onto but into the garden. Large urns of rosemary (left) and bay (right) stand on either side of the path in the foreground. The central knot-garden, as shown in diagram below, measures 12 by 12 feet; the entire garden, above, measures 22 by 12 feet.

Plants

Plants most suitable for a knot-garden are: gray and green santolina, germander (*Teucrium chamadrys*), thrift or seapinks (*Armeria maritima alba* or *Armeria maritima lauchreana*), rue (*Ruta graveolens*), hyssop (*Hyssopus officinalis*), lavender (*Munstead* variety) or English thyme (*Thymus vulgaris*). For closed knots, to accent the inbetween spaces, choose lamb's ear (*Stachys lanata* or *Byzantina*) or silver-leafed Veronica (*Veronica incana*). Creeping thyme (particularly woolly thyme) may be planted as a ground cover to cascade over the edge of the bed onto the walkway.

Legend

- Woolly Thyme (Thymus lanuginosus)
- Thrift (Maritima alba or Maritima lauchreana),
- Germander (Teucrium senescens var. glaucum)
- Blue Mound and Common Rue (Ruta graveolens species)
- Lamb's Ear (Stachys lanata or Byzantina)
- Circle Onion (Allium senescens var. glaucum)

A garden should be seen as an extension of the house—as an outdoor room connected by a walkway. You should be able to view a garden through a window looking out as well as from the outside looking toward the house. The right kind of enclosure, a wall or fence, will complete the "outdoor room" as an architectural link between house and garden. The sundial garden, in diagram below, measures 24 by 25 feet and is the center of the larger garden, left, which measures 50 by 100 feet.

18th-Century-style Herb Garden

Layout

A typical 18th-century-style garden is created by two walkways intersecting each other, a concept which can be traced back to Sumerian gardens, 3000 B.C. With a definite center established, four beds are formed around it, separated by the walkways. (See diagram below.) To highlight the center, a fountain, sculpture, tree or, as shown, a sundial may be placed in the exact center of a circular bed or a square or diamond-shaped bed.

Walkways

In this style garden, walkways serve a visual as well as a practical purpose. By separating raised beds (raised for better drainage), access is given to all areas for weeding and harvesting. Walkways may be laid in brick, stone or gravel by using a landscape fabric beneath for weed control. Beds, too, can be covered with landscape fabric, with holes cut for the plantings, then obscured under a thin layer of gravel. This is helpful for two reasons: In winter, it provides extra protection against frost, and during the summer months, less watering is needed.

Soil

A light soil with a course texture is ideal for most herb plants. Add gravel, sand and peat moss to your garden soil. Use fertilizer (dehydrated cow manure) sparingly. Overly rich soil will cause winter-kill or lush foliage with little fragrance. Most herbs need an alkaline soil, so add lime.

A boxwood border on four adjacent beds, interplanted with a variety of herbs, including purple sage and foxglove as shown above, adds continuity in all seasons.

Legend

- Sundial
- Square Planters
- Lamb's Ear (Stachys Byzantina)
- Silver Mound (Artemisia Schmidtiana)
- Lemon Thyme (Thymus citriodorus)
- Purple Sage (Salvia officinalis var.)
- Foxglove (Digitalis ambigua)
- Lavender (Lavendula angustifolia)
- True English Dwarf Boxwood (Buxus sempervirens suffruticosa)
- Camphor-scented Southernwood (Artemisia abrotanum var. camphorata)

Gifts from Gardeners

In fact, most of these gifts from nature are as appropriate for a gardener as they are thoughtful gifts a gardener might prepare for someone else.

Herb Sampler

Bouquet Garni (recipe is on this page)
Thread
Gift tags
Wide ribbon
Scissors
Long piece of narrow ribbon

Tie gift tags around Bouquets Garni with thread, and label each one for vegetables, for meat, etc.

Sew bundles to a wide ribbon and tie on a small pair of scissors with a long ribbon so the cook can snip off the little bundles when needed.

Grapefruit Bird Baskets

Baskets made from hollowed-out grapefruit and filled with food birds like are a thoughtful gift to neighborhood birds, especially when snow covers the ground and food is hard to find.

1 grapefruit
¾ cup suet, softened
1 cup birdseed
String

Slice grapefruit in half and scoop out juice and pulp completely. Make a hole on each side to accommodate a string for hanging. Place in a 275F oven for 3 to 4 hours until firm and dry or dry in a microwave oven for 6 minutes at lowest setting. Mix suet with birdseed and generously fill each half of grapefruit. Thread a string through holes and hang outside near a window.

Bouquet Garni

Cheesecloth
Dried herbs (see Hint)
Thread

Cut cheesecloth into 4-inch squares. Mix herbs together and place 1 teaspoon of mixture in center of each square. Bring corners together and wrap and tie securely with thread. Makes 4.

For meat, blend 1 teaspoon each of nutmeg, thyme, chervil and tarragon; for fish, blend 1 teaspoon each of tarragon, mint, dill and lemon peel; and for sauces, soups, stews and vegetables, use 4 bay leaves, 1 teaspoon thyme and 2 teaspoons parsley.

Dream Bags

Calico
Thread
Sweet Dreams Potpourri (recipe below)
Ribbon

Sew little bags of calico. Stuff with potpourri and tie tightly with ribbon. Place under pillows for sweet dreams.

Sweet Dreams Potpourri

1 cup dried rosemary
1 cup dried lemon verbena
2 cups dried pine needles
Lavender or rose oil or perfume

Crush and mix together rosemary, lemon verbena and pine needles. Add a drop of lavender or rose oil or, if oils are unavailable, a drop of perfume.

Bay Leaf Wreath

No. 28- or 32-gauge wire
Foundation wreath of straw wound with
  nylon thread
Bay leaves
Heavy-duty green thread
Variety of dried flowers (optional)
Ribbon (optional)

Wrap wire around foundation wreath and make a loop for hanging. String bay leaves on thread and wrap around wreath, placing leaves carefully. Repeat until wreath is covered. Add other dried flowers and a ribbon, if desired.

Recipe Collection

Transplant a healthy herb or flowering plant into an attractive pot. Write your favorite recipes clearly on index cards (you might want to try your hand at calligraphy for the recipe titles) and tie around the plant with a ribbon.

Gardener's Basket

Fill a rattan harvesting basket with an assortment of fruit, vegetable and flower seeds. Add a shiny new trowel and a pair of gardening gloves or knee pads.

Garden Markers

Styrofoam from meat or produce trays
Waterproof felt-tip markers
Waterproof glue
Garden stakes or small dowels

Cut out flower and vegetable shapes from Styrofoam and color with markers. Glue to stakes and use to mark garden rows.

Chili Ristras

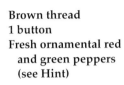

Brown thread
1 button
Fresh ornamental red
  and green peppers
  (see Hint)

Cut a piece of thread about a yard long. Tie a button on one end to prevent the peppers from falling off. String peppers on thread and allow enough thread left over to make a loop for hanging. Hang to dry.

Peppers contain capsaicin, an irritant to skin and eyes. Work with rubber gloves outside or in a well-ventilated place.

Garlic Wreath

This is a gift that any good cook will treasure, and use!

Late in October, pull garlic bulbs from the soil. Braid stems and leaves and tie ends together to make a wreath. Hang to dry. Wreath should last a year.

April in December

Spring flowers make perfect winter gifts and forcing bulbs is not at all difficult if you follow directions carefully. When choosing varieties for forcing, check with your local florist or nursery to pick ones that are adaptable. Bulbs may be potted in containers of several different sizes: standard, three-quarter or half. Bulbs require a medium potting soil to which compost has been added. The pointed tips of the bulbs should show above soil level.

A few varieties, hyacinth and paper-white narcissus, for example, can be forced in water as well as soil. Special bowls are available for this purpose. Paper-whites can also be forced in a pebble-filled bowl. Press bulbs into pebbles so that they almost touch each other and add water to just cover pebbles. Add a piece of charcoal to each dish to keep the water clear and delay bacterial formation and growth. Maintain water level just below bottom.

All bulbs need a period of darkness and relatively cool temperatures in order to form root systems. See the chart below for time and temperature requirements. After roots have formed, bulbs should be moved gradually into sunlight to develop top growth and flowers. Start bulbs at different times and you'll have fresh flowers all winter.

Forcing Spring Bulbs for Winter Blossoms

Flower	Best Planting Time	Pot	Weeks To Root	Weeks To Force	Temperature Nights & Cloudy Days	Fragrant
Amaryllis	Nov. to Dec.	Standard pot	4 to 6	8 to 12	65F and over	No
Calla lily, yellow	Nov. to Dec.	Standard pot	4	12 to 14	65F and over	No
Cape lily	September	Standard pot	4	6 to 8	60 to 65F	No
Daffodil	October	½ or ¾ pot	6 to 8	8	55 to 60F	Yes
Freesia	Aug. to Oct.	½ pot or flat	6	12 to 14	50 to 55F	Yes
Hyacinth, Dutch	October	½, ¾ or standard pot	6 to 8	4 to 6	50 to 55F	Yes
Hyacinth, French and Roman	Sept. to Oct.	Bowl or pot	4 to 6	6 to 8	55 to 60F	Yes
Iris	September	½ pot	4	6 to 10	55 to 60F	No
Lily, Easter	November	Standard pot	6 to 8	8 to 12	60F and over	Yes
Narcissus, paper-white	Oct. to Nov.	Bowl	1 to 4	5 to 10	55 to 60F	Yes
Shamrock	Sept. to Oct.	Bowl or ½ pot	4	8	65F and over	No

Planting Flowers for Cutting

Popular cutting annuals include cornflowers, snapdragons, marigolds, larkspur (an annual delphinium), salvia, cosmos, petunias, zinnias and asters. Tubers such as gladiola, tuberoses and dahlias will make good cutting flowers.

Some perennials—peonies, delphinium, monkshood, hybrid lilies, chrysanthemums, baby's breath, roses, liatris, as well as flowering bulbs such as tulips, daffodils and hyacinth—are also favorites for cutting.

Both annuals and perennials come in a variety of heights, colors and blooming times. Check seed catalogs and ask your supplier for advice about the most wilt-resistant strains and find out what will grow best in your area. Depending on the climate, a cutting garden can provide material for 5 to 12 months a year.

Preparing Fresh Flowers

When you cut the stem of a flower, the cells at the cut begin to close up, so the stem cannot absorb water. Thirsty flowers droop and die.

Take a pail with water in it to the garden; strip unwanted foliage from the stems of cut flowers and place the flowers into water up to, but not over, the foliage and blossoms for display.

Arranging: Making an attractive arrangement takes practice. Like any artist, you will develop your own style. Here are some very basic tips to get started:

❀ Don't force flowers into a preconceived notion of what your arrangement should look like. Instead, let the materials' most attractive properties inspire the final design.

❀ Work with three types of materials: outline material to define the shape of the arrangement, focus material for a visual "hero" and filler.

❀ Experiment with contrasts: light and dark shades, soft and hard lines and rough and shiny textures.

❀ Keep the size of your container and the size range of materials within the arrangement in proportion to one another.

❀ Try unusual color combinations. Freely mixing nature's colors creates the excitement of a summer garden in your display.

❀ Don't overcrowd your arrangement. Less is more. Give each flower or spray breathing space. The blossoms should not support each other.

When you buy cut flowers or prepare your own, follow these steps:

- Ask your florist for a packet of preservative to add to the water. It contains sugar, citric acid and a bactericide to help the stems absorb water and retard growth of bacteria.

🌱 *To make a homemade preservative with all the benefits of a commercial preservative, mix 1 part lemon-based beverage (such as 7-Up or Sprite—don't use diet soda) to 3 parts water; add a few drops of bleach.*

- Mix preservative with warm, not cold, water to aid absorption.

- Protect flowers from extreme cold. Even a few minutes in freezing temperatures can kill them.

- Strip away foliage that will be below the waterline.

- Trim 1 inch off stem on diagonal with a sharp knife (scissors may crush stems).

- Place stems in water immediately after cutting so they can absorb water before air seals cut ends.

- To kill damaging bacteria, wash the inside of the container and other objects that will be in contact with flowers in mild dish soap and a small amount of bleach. Rinse thoroughly before filling the container.

Containers and Mechanics

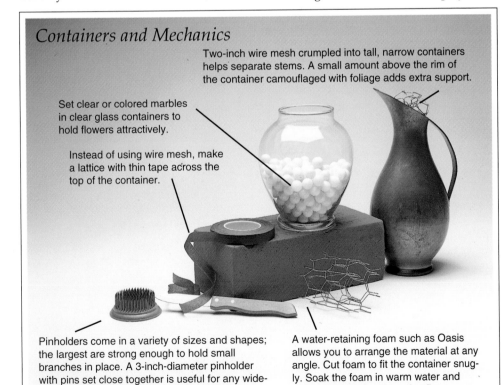

Two-inch wire mesh crumpled into tall, narrow containers helps separate stems. A small amount above the rim of the container camouflaged with foliage adds extra support.

Set clear or colored marbles in clear glass containers to hold flowers attractively.

Instead of using wire mesh, make a lattice with thin tape across the top of the container.

Pinholders come in a variety of sizes and shapes; the largest are strong enough to hold small branches in place. A 3-inch-diameter pinholder with pins set close together is useful for any wide-mouth container. Use double-sided florist's tape to anchor the pinholder to the container.

A water-retaining foam such as Oasis allows you to arrange the material at any angle. Cut foam to fit the container snugly. Soak the foam in warm water and preservative before inserting flowers.

Basket Weaving

Both experienced and novice basket weavers will enjoy this project and the lovely heart-shaped breakfast basket on page 96. The basic weaving techniques are easy to master and both baskets, as you can see, are as functional as they are pretty.

To make this old-fashioned egg basket, you first form a crossed frame by fitting a 6-inch wooden hoop across the inside of a 6-inch grapevine wreath, then weave modified god's-eyes (see page 95) at either end where the hoop and grapevine intersect. Insert six pointed spokes into the god's-eyes on each end to complete the frame for the bottom and simply fill the frame in with reed weavers and decorative narrow grapevines or dyed reed.

Reed for baskets is sold in 1-pound coils at craft and hobby shops or may be ordered by mail. You can get eight 6-inch baskets out of a 1-pound coil of reed. Invite some friends to chip in and make baskets together. Borrow from the fun and friendship of a quilting bee—have a basket bee!

Gather natural grapevine "green" in late spring through early fall; while sap is still in the vine it will be pliable.

One 6' length of grapevine, about ¼" diameter, to coil into a 6"-diameter wreath for frame

Two 6' lengths of ⅛" grapevine for dark weavers (optional)

One 1-lb coil no. 3 round reed for weavers (about 82' per basket)

6" wooden hoop, ½" wide

One 1-lb coil no. 6 round reed to cut 2 lengths each 10¼", 9¼" and 9¾" for spokes, tips shaved to points with knife or sharpener (about 9' per basket)

Tape measure; sharp knife or tin snips and pencil sharpener; small screwdriver or awl

1. Soak all grapevines overnight in a sink or tub of water to make them pliable. From the coil of no. 3 round reed cut five lengths, each about 6 feet long, and soak for at least 20 minutes before using. Make a 6-inch loop in the center of the ¼-inch grapevine. Thread one free end through the loop and bend it around the loop, tucking the tip inside to hold the shape of a circle as shown in photo. Repeat with other free end and trim tips flush, if necessary. Fit the wooden hoop inside wreath across its center at right angles to form a frame and handle. Hold them together by weaving modified god's-eyes at each end with 6-foot lengths of no. 3 round reed made pliable by soaking.

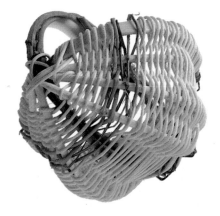

2. 9¼"   2. 9¼"
1. 10¼"   1. 10¼"
3. 9¾"   3. 9¾"

2. Poke a channel between strands of woven reed with a small screwdriver or awl so you can insert the points of the no. 6 round reed spokes into the god's-eyes on either end. This makes a frame for the bottom, evenly spaced on either side of the vine.

Modified god's-eye

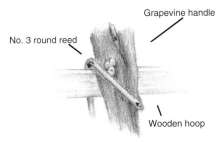

Grapevine handle

No. 3 round reed

Wooden hoop

1. Pinch one end of no. 3 reed inside basket against flat side of hoop so tip pokes upward ½ inch above top of hoop behind grapevine. Pull other end snugly under hoop, up diagonally across vine on outside, then down over top edge of hoop on inside.

2. Pull reed down against bottom of hoop, then pass it up diagonally again over vine on outside and back down inside basket, catching tip under reed to hold in place against hoop.

3. Pull reed down and around vine on outside below hoop. Loop it up around hoop inside, then around vine under hoop to the other side again.

4. Continue until there are six loops on each side and six loops around vine below hoop. Repeat at other end of basket.

3. Fill in the bottom by weaving five rows of no. 3 round reed back and forth around the hoop on each side, passing alternately over and under the spokes of no. 6 reed. Weave three rows of ⅛-inch grapevine in the same way, on each side. (Thin grapevine tends to break easily. Dye 12 feet of no. 3 round reed dark brown to substitute for the grapevine weavers if you wish.) Finish filling bottom by weaving no. 3 round reed all the way across as shown in photo. Tuck tips in. To connect a new length of reed to the end of a woven one, overlap their tip ends about ½ inch next to each other over a spoke on inside of basket. Trim tips that protrude more than ¼ inch inside basket.

A 9-inch basket shaped like this can hold lots of loving surprises. Natural reed is usually sold in 1-pound coils—enough to make about eight similar baskets. Amounts given for each basket in materials list are approximate.

1 lb ½" flat reed (24' needed)
1 lb ¼" flat oval reed (33' needed)
1 lb ¼" flat reed (12' needed)
1 lb no. 3 round reed (7' optional)
Spring-type clothespins; tape measure; sharp knife or scissors
Colorfast fabric dye (optional)

Flat reed has a right and wrong side. The wrong side, when bent, will fray and the right side will remain smooth. Weave the basket with the right side of the flat reed on the side that will most often be seen.

1. From the ½-inch flat reed, cut ten 18-inch and six 15-inch lengths. Fasten each group together with a clothespin. From the ¼-inch flat oval reed, cut 10 lengths about 1 yard long. Cut ¼-inch flat reed into two 6-foot lengths. Soak all pieces in water for at least 15 minutes before weaving them.

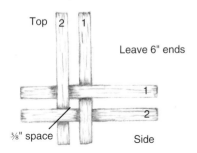

Top 2 1

Leave 6" ends

1
2

⅜" space   Side

2. Start with four of the 18-inch lengths. Measure 6 inches in from one end and begin weaving at this point in an over/under fashion (like a lattice pie crust) with the first four weavers. Leave a ⅜-inch square space between each weaver.

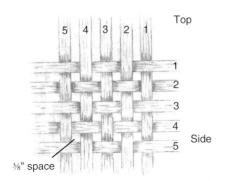

Top
5 4 3 2 1

1
2
3
4
5

⅜" space   Side

3. Continue weaving the other six weavers in an over/under pattern, alternating each new weaver between top and side, and leaving 6-inch ends unwoven. The 10 weavers should form a square. If the reeds have started to dry out, place them in water to soak for 5 minutes.

4. Continue to weave three of the 15-inch lengths from the right side in the over/under pattern over the five weavers until a total of eight rows are woven, leaving 6 inches unwoven at the beginning of each weaver.

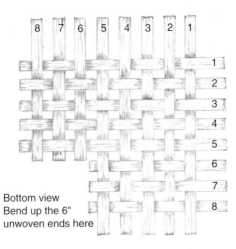

8 7 6 5 4 3 2 1

1
2
3
4
5
6
7
8

Bottom view
Bend up the 6"
unwoven ends here

5. To complete the base of the heart basket, weave rows 6, 7 and 8 with the last three 15-inch lengths over and under from the top, weaving over *only five* of the side weavers to form an inverted L. This completes the base.

6. Gently bend up all the free 6-inch ends and clothespin three or four weavers together, in preparation for weaving the sides. Place the basket back in the water for 5 minutes.

7. Tuck tip of one length of ¼-inch flat oval reed, oval side out, under one of the base reeds. Thread the other end over and under the base reeds all around the bottom side, as shown in photo below. Overlap ends about 3 inches and trim tip to hide it. Weave seven more rows in the same way, starting each row at a different point around side. Substitute dyed reed for top four rows, if desired.

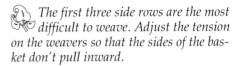

The first three side rows are the most difficult to weave. Adjust the tension on the weavers so that the sides of the basket don't pull inward.

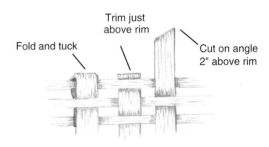

Trim just
above rim

Fold and tuck

Cut on angle
2" above rim

8. To finish the rim, soak basket and flat reed for 5 minutes. Trim 6-inch ends protruding from top of basket alternately flush and 2 inches long, as shown above. Bend the 2-inch lengths inside the basket and tuck the angled tip inside the top row of ¼-inch reed.

9. Cut two pieces of ¼-inch flat oval reed 1½ inches longer than the circumference of the rim of the basket. Use clothespins at 2-inch intervals to hold in place on either side of the rim with oval faces out. Overlap ends.

Inside rim

Outside rim

10. Bind the rim with two 6-foot lengths of ¼-inch flat reed: Tuck end of one length, with its wrong side down, in between basket and inner rim at top of heart. Thread other end through the closest opening, then over the top of the rim to the inside and out through the next opening. Bind all the way around to the beginning; then, using second 6-foot length, reverse direction to make crisscross binding. Fasten end by tucking it inside rim. Wet basket thoroughly and mold it into a heart shape with your hands before it dries.

Weaving Wheat

Creating symbolic and decorative figures from wheat and other grains has been a harvest-season custom all over the world since primitive times. It was believed that the forces of death and rebirth lived in the crops of the field and that the last pieces of grain harvested housed these spirits.

To keep the spirits safe until it was once again time to plant, the harvesters used the last sheaf of the harvest to make woven designs or decorative bundles. These figures were called "corn dollies," although they rarely took on human form. Often corn dollies assumed traditional symbolic shapes, and it appears that the word *doll* is a modification of the word *idol*. The corn dollies, traditionally thought to be blessed by Ceres, the goddess of the harvest, were kept indoors during the winter and cast into the fields in the spring to help nourish the new crops.

Other woven objects, called straw favors, were crafted by farmers and given to their sweethearts as tokens of affection. Weave your own straw favors like the Braided Harvest Twist shown above on the top of a vintage Shredded Wheat crate. Present them to friends to wish them a harvest of good fortune.

You don't have to live in the heartland or wait until autumn to practice this lovely tradition. Prepared straw can be purchased at craft stores, and you might even try paper straw which can be painted or dyed to produce a variety of colorful designs. Whatever straw you use should have a hollow center.

We've provided instructions for braiding and plaiting in the two projects here. Once you have mastered these two simple weaving techniques, you can create any number of other original designs. You will need the following materials and tools for either project:

Heads of wheat or barley, with long stems
   (dried well)
Large flat pan of warm water
Terry cloth towel
Old scissors (not good fabric scissors)
Stout thread in straw color
12" lengths of ¼" ribbon
Small lengths of raffia or thread (for loops
   to hang wheat weaving up)

Although wheat is by far the most popular choice, oats, rye, barley and maize also work nicely. If dried properly, straw can be stored for years in a dry place to prevent it from becoming moldy. Before you begin working you should separate your straw into groups of short, medium and longer stem sizes.

Here's another arrangement you can make with braided or plaited wheat. Make a plain bundle of wheat heads, with 3 to 4 inches of stem attached, and decorate it with separate braids of straw in single or double loops.

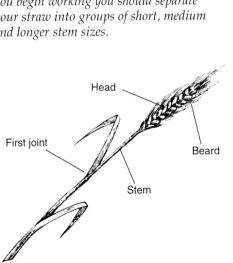

Head
First joint
Beard
Stem

Braided Harvest Twist

1. Cut wheat stalks just above the first joint so that you have the heads with the long, perfectly smooth stems attached.

2. Soak straw for 20 minutes in luke-warm water. Remove a piece and bend it gently; if it is pliable and does not crack, it is ready to use. If not, return it to the water for 10 more minutes. When the straw is ready, wrap it in a terry cloth towel and leave for 15 minutes. Remove only as much as you need to work with and leave the rest in the towel. Any straw left over from a project should be spread out to dry so it will not mildew.

3. Choose six evenly matched heads and leave three of them in the towel.

(Continued from page 99.)

4. Tie three of the straws together with thread just below the heads. Braid in a simple three-strand braid to a length of 5 to 6 inches. Tie to hold. Repeat the braiding process with the other three straws.

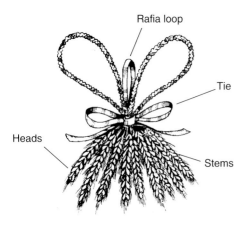

5. Form each braid into a loop and lay the two loops side by side so that all ties are together. Tie again. Cover tie with a ribbon bow, adding a short loop of raffia for hanging.

6. Trim straw ends to attractive lengths and spread these and heads to form a fan. Dry thoroughly.

Plaited Harvest Heart
Follow steps 1 and 2 for Braided Harvest Twist.

Plaiting the Strips
1. Choose eight well-matched heads with long stems. Leave four in the towel and work with the other four. With the thread, tie these together just below the heads.

2. Turn bundle so that heads face down and stems (straws) are up. Spread the straws out to form a cross and hold flat with your left thumb (reverse this if you are left-handed). With one arm of

the cross pointing directly toward you (the bottom straw), bend the top (opposite) straw toward you, folding it flat so it lies parallel to the bottom one. Fold the bottom one upward to the top position. Press both flat and repeat this process with the left and right straws.

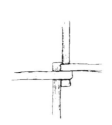

3. Continue this sequence of bending first one and then the other set of straws until the plait is 4 to 5 inches long. Tie the end with thread and return the strip to the towel.

4. Repeat steps 2 and 3 with the other four long straws, making a second plaited strip 4 to 5 inches long.

Making the Heart
1. Cut three more straws to equal lengths, about 6 to 7 inches long below the heads.

2. With straw-colored thread, tie the ends of the two plaited strips to the center of the bundle of three straws,

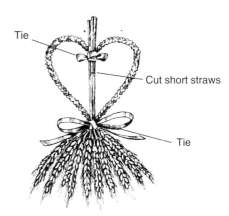

with the heads of the plaited strips facing upward and the other heads facing down. Bend the plaited strips over and tie them again where the thread holds them just below the heads. This will form a heart shape, with all the heads in a spray at its base. Include in the tie all those straws from the plaited strips which are long enough to reach. Cut short ones just below the first tie.

3. Tie the ribbon at the base of the heart just above the heads, forming a neat bow. Trim ribbon ends evenly.

4. Put the finished favor in an airy place to dry completely.

Vary the heart design by tying the plaits to the center in the opposite direction and adding three tiny heads at that tie.

Make several loops of varying sizes and add them to the basic Harvest Twist. Depending on the size of the finished piece, leave the heads on or cut them off.

ew designs will suggest them-selves as you work with straw. By experimenting with your own ideas, you can create an endless number of objects. Straw weaving techniques can be utilized to make mobiles, Christmas tree ornaments, cheerful kitchen decorations, table centerpieces, wholesome housewarming gifts and clever gift-wrap adornments, as we've shown here. Tie one on top of a loaf of fresh-baked bread for a new neighbor or decorate a baby gift (wheat is a symbol of fertility).

Your choice of ribbon color can also send a special message to your friends: Traditionally a red ribbon symbolizes warmth; green is for spring and fertility; blue indicates truth; yellow is for the corn and the goddess Ceres; white symbolizes purity; and brown represents the earth.

Cornhusk Doll

The best cornhusks are those dried on stalks in the fields, but if you don't happen to live in corn country, cornhusks from the ears of corn bought at the market make fine dolls. Save the fine-grained inner husks closest to the corn cob and lay them out on newspapers or screens to dry in the sun (save some cornsilk, too, for hair). As they dry they are bleached to a soft oat color and will wrinkle and curl somewhat, but rest assured they will flatten again as you work.

20 cornhusks, plus extras for any accessories
Large pan or pail of warm water
Heavy-duty cotton thread or string
White glue
Cornsilk, lamb's wool or raveled yarn (for hair)

Be sure to use cotton thread as synthetic thread will stretch. Fresh cornhusks (not dried) will curl up as they dry, ruining the doll made from them. Cornhusks dried in a bunch on the doll instead of separately (all spread out) are also likely to mildew.

Making the Doll

1. Soak 13 dried husks in warm water for a few minutes to soften them, then lay them all out on a towel. This helps to keep husks from splitting and makes them easier to work with.

2. Cut off the puckered part that was attached to the base of the cob and the tip of the pointed end, making each husk almost rectangular.

3. Select the two smoothest husks and put them together, one atop the other. Take two more husks and place the smooth husks between them, making a sandwich with the smooth husks as filling. With cotton thread, tie all four husks firmly ¾ inch from the top end.

4. Reverse the bunch so that the tied top is at the bottom; peel down strips of husk over the knot (as though you were peeling a banana) so that the bunch is turned inside out. The knot will then be on the inside and the best husks will be on the outside.

5. Notice which husk is the best looking and turn it last, pulling it around the others to form a smooth face. Stretch this husk around to form a distinct chin (the pucker in the top will be covered with hair). Tie neck securely.

6. Braid three cornhusks together tightly, tying at both ends of braid. Tie a cornhusk over the thread at each end to hide it. Thread this arm piece through middle of doll, between front and back husks and just beneath tied neck.

7. Take two husks and fold one over each shoulder, crossing them at doll's waist and tying at the waist.

8. Select husks for the skirt. You will need three or more, depending how full you wish the skirt to be. Soak and trim husks as in steps 1 and 2. For a doll with narrow hips, tie husks on directly at waist and tie a narrow strip of wet cornhusk around the waist to cover thread and husk ends. Allow strip to dry completely before trimming, or leave ends long, like apron ties.

9. For a full skirt, tie husks onto waist, upside down, then peel husks down over the tie. Trim bottom of skirt so it is even. Test by standing the doll up.

10. Smooth white glue on head (but not on the face!). Add a tangle of dried cornsilk, lamb's wool or raveled yarn and pat it down into the glue. Allow to dry before adding a bonnet.

11. Wrap a husk over the top of the head, exposing the face and front of the hair, to make a bonnet. Fold from each side toward center of back so the folds meet at back of neck. Tie with thread around neck to secure, then hide thread with a strip of husk. Trim ends of bonnet husk ½ inch below tie.

12. While her arms are still damp, tie or wire them into the position you wish them to stay in. When doll is dry, remove ties or wire and arms will remain in place.

Thistle Mouse

Tillie Teasel bustles busily through her daily chores, never leaving a surface undusted, a plate unwashed or a brass lamp unpolished. She learned to keep an impeccable house from the good, hardworking Appalachian folks who made her and lots of her relatives from the common teasel that grows so plentifully in West Virginia.

Teasel creatures, including mice like Tillie, were probably made as inexpensive gifts to entertain children. Whether you're partial to country mice or city mice, you'll find that this traditional Appalachian critter will be a perfect permanent guest in your own home (as quiet as a you-know-what) or a great gift for a friend who appreciates whimsical charm.

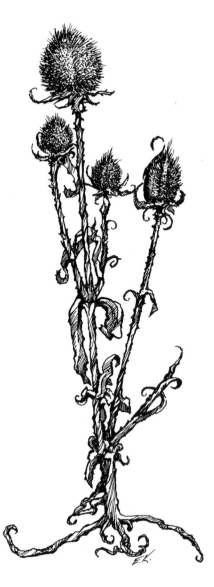

¼ yard calico fabric
Sewing thread to match fabric
Small amount dried beans (no more than 1 cup)
Small amount cotton batting
Dried teasel
⅓ yard lace, ¼" wide
Craft glue (optional)
⅛ yard lace, 2" wide
½ yard ribbon, ⅛" wide
2 black map pins
Compass; pencil

1. With compass draw two circles on calico, one 8 inches in diameter (for the bottom) and the other 7 inches in diameter (for the head). Cut both out.

2. Make one row of gathering stitches around perimeter of 8-inch circle, ¼ inch from edge. Pull thread to gather fabric into a pouch but leave an opening. Fill with dried beans; cover beans and finish filling with cotton batting. Close by gathering tightly and knotting thread.

3. Gather 7-inch circle, ¼ inch from edge. Fill partially with cotton batting. Cut dried teasel from stem, leaving at least ¼ inch of stem attached. Place teasel in batting, leaving stem end showing. Adjust cotton batting so that the teasel protrudes from fabric and looks like a face with a bonnet on its head.

4. Cut a 1- by 8-inch strip of fabric for arms. Fold in half lengthwise, right sides together. Sew long edge closed with ¼-inch seam allowance. Sew or glue ¼-inch lace to ends for cuffs. Turn right side out. Glue arms to body.

5. Attach head to bottom with a few slip stitches. Glue or sew ¼-inch lace on bonnet to frame face.

6. Cut 2-inch lace to size for apron. Stitch a piece of ⅛-inch-wide ribbon to each side of apron for ties, then tie around mouse. Tie a bow around bonnet and also around neck if desired. Insert map pins for eyes.

Appalachian crafters are also fond of teasel hedgehogs and make them with plain teasels on a driftwood base. Play with your hedgehog or mouse, using scraps of materials and adapting the general instructions for constructing Thistle Mouse. Teasel creatures are decorative, but were originally constructed as playthings for children, so use your imagination and play. That's what makes them fun. Thistle Mouse can be transformed into Thistle Hedgehog with some basic alterations. The following additional materials are needed:

2 pieces pinecone for ears
2 sequins for eyes
Tiny piece driftwood for base
Black felt-tip pen

Make the teasel mouse face, but don't dress the body up in clothes. Allow it to lie flat on the driftwood base. Add ears, eyes and mark a black nose with felt-tip marker, using our art as a guide.

The mature fruit of the fuller's teasel, with its flexible spines and curved barbs, was used to "tease" or raise the nap on wool. The wire device now used by the textile industry to do the same job is still called a teasel. Teasels grow wild in many parts of the country and are often used in dried flower arrangements. If you can't find teasels to pick yourself, you can purchase teasels from a florist or crafts shop that sells materials for dried arrangements.

Fragrant Settings

Flowers have always played an important role at weddings, but the simple splendor of floral decoration isn't limited to fresh flowers or to the actual wedding day celebration. If you're planning a shower, bridal luncheon or any special event that calls for a romantic look, herbs and dried flowers can be just as lovely and appropriate as fresh blossoms. The table accents above combine fragrant stalks of eucalyptus, dried roses and rosebuds, and sprigs of baby's breath.

Early Roman brides carried clusters of herbs under their veils as a symbol of their fidelity. Bridesmaids' bouquets originally contained pungent herbs to drive evil spirits away from the bridal couple.

The appeal of this ensemble of table accents is its tasteful simplicity and versatility. Each element is simple to construct and can easily be used with or without the other elements, depending on your needs. If you're planning a lawn party, cover your picnic table with a white or pink cloth and add swags and a Wreath Centerpiece for alfresco elegance. Yellow roses make equally attractive accents and are perfect with more informal yellow picnic linens or tableware.

You can dry roses and rosebuds by hanging them in a warm, dry area, or use silica gel (see page 41). The materials listed here will be enough to make the items shown in the picture, opposite. The number of roses and rosebuds and the amount of baby's breath you'll need depend on individual taste. We used seven roses and about twelve rosebuds in the Wreath Centerpiece. The flowers, including the baby's breath, should be used sparingly so that your accents are airy, not cluttered.

2 bunches of eucalyptus, 1 lb each
14" crimped metal ring
2 metal rings, 4" each
Dried roses
Dried rosebuds
Dried baby's breath
12' of no. 6 florist's wire
Place cards
Glue gun
Cutters suitable for cutting eucalyptus

Before you begin working with the eucalyptus, save two long stalks (at least 12 inches) for the swags. Use the medium-size pieces for the Wreath Centerpiece and Sweetheart Bobeches, and save smaller pieces for the Sweetheart Napkin Rings and Decorative Place Cards.

Clip stems off rosebuds and leave small (about 1 inch) stems on roses.

Wreath Centerpiece

1. Cut eucalyptus into 6-inch pieces. Cut a 2-foot piece of florist's wire.
2. Gather together five pieces of eucalyptus. Hold the eucalyptus on top of the 14-inch metal ring with one hand and with the other hand secure eucalyptus to ring by tightly wrapping the

Eucalyptus, shown in the swag above, is grown in California and Australia, then cut and preserved with glycerin. It is sold at flower and craft shops.

wire around both eucalyptus and ring about three times.
3. Gather five more pieces of eucalyptus and place on top of the wire ring, covering the bottom of the previously attached eucalyptus. Secure eucalyptus to the metal ring as described in step 2.
4. Continue attaching eucalyptus to the ring in this manner until you have completely covered the metal ring.

When you use up the 2-foot piece of wire, cut another 2-foot piece and continue wrapping where you left off. You may need two or three pieces of wire to complete the ring.

5. When the ring is completely covered with eucalyptus, experiment with placement of rosebuds, roses and baby's breath. When you have gotten the desired effect, use the glue gun to attach rosebuds directly onto eucalyptus leaves. Next, glue small sprigs of baby's breath to the ring, and finally glue six or seven dried roses onto eucalyptus to complete the ring.

Sweetheart Bobeches

1. For each bobeche, cut eucalyptus into 3-inch pieces. Cut a 1-foot piece of wire.
2. Gather together three pieces of eucalyptus. Hold the eucalyptus on top of a 4-inch metal ring with one hand while tightly wrapping the wire around both eucalyptus and ring about three times.

3. Continue this process until the ring is covered with eucalyptus.
4. Glue rosebuds and sprigs of baby's breath to the eucalyptus leaves with the glue gun.

Eucalyptus Swag

Cut a 12-inch piece of eucalyptus. Glue rosebuds and baby's breath to the eucalyptus and your swag is finished. We used two swags for the table pictured, opposite.

Sweetheart Napkin Rings

1. For each ring, wrap an 8-inch piece of eucalyptus around itself to form a circle about 2 inches in diameter. Using a small piece of wire, secure the ends of the eucalyptus together.
2. Randomly glue rosebuds to the eucalyptus leaves, and attach one dried rose to the circle, creating a decorative top to your napkin ring.

Decorative Place Cards

Choose plain, elegant place cards. You may find it easier, especially if you're left-handed, to write the names of your guests on each card before adding your accents.

Glue a 1½-inch sprig of eucalyptus to the upper left corner of the place card. Add a sprig of baby's breath and some rosebuds to complete the motif.

Picture Guide to Culinary and Medicinal Herbs

As you use the various herbs called for in our recipes, you may wish to look at this chart and find out what the plants look like, what some of their reputed medicinal uses are and any other names they might also be known by.

The information given here on traditional therapeutic uses of herbs derives mostly from ancient medical custom and folk wisdom. Whether or not they work depends on whom you ask.

Anise *(Pimpinella anisum)*
Other name: Anise Seed
A delicate, sprawling plant with spindly shaped seeds.
Ancient uses: Placed on the pillow, anise was believed to prevent bad dreams. Pliny recommended it as a breath freshener, to be chewed and followed by rinsing the mouth with wine.

Bay Tree *(Laurus nobibis)*
Other names: Laurel, Sweet Bay
An evergreen that may reach 30 feet tall, with small leaves and oval berries.
Ancient uses: The Greeks and Romans favored laurel wreaths to honor important people. The expressions "poet laureate" and "look to your laurels" reflect this origin. Bay tree tea, which had a narcotic effect, was also enjoyed.

Basil *(Ocimum basilicum)*
Other name: Sweet Basil
An annual with a clovelike scent that produces a profusion of flowers.
Ancient uses: When used for snuff, basil was once credited with allaying "nervous headache." Pots of basil kept all around the house were said to drive away flies and witches.

Bergamot *(Monarda didyma)*
Other names: Bee Balm, Oswego Tea
A perennial with hollow stems and brilliant scarlet flowers.
Ancient uses: The Oswego Indians of New York introduced bergamot-stem tea to the colonists. It was reputed to induce relaxation and sleep.

Caraway *(Carum carvi)*
Other name: Caraway Seed
A feathery foliaged biennial with tiny white flowers, grown primarily for its spindle-shaped seeds.
Ancient uses: Caraway was once believed to be a cure for baldness, restoring long-gone hair growth. Today the oil is used to flavor medications.

Cardamom *(Elettaria cardamomum)*
Other name: Malabar Cardamom
A large, dark-green perennial bearing aromatic capsular fruit.
Ancient uses: Cardamom was traditionally credited with relieving stomach ailments. In Europe the seeds were used as a breath sweetener, often dispensed at bars so imbibers could cover up their telltale breath.

Cayenne *(Capsicum minimum)*
Other names: Chilies, Red Pepper, Bird Pepper
A brilliant-green herb with elongated, pungent red fruits.
Ancient uses: In the past, cayenne was lauded as a strong and reliable stimulant, as well as a remedy for cardiac ailments. "Full of pepper" is also a euphemism for obnoxiousness when used to describe someone.

Celery *(Apium graveolens)*
Other names: Smallage, Wild Celery
A familiar vegetable of the carrot family, grown also for its seeds.
Ancient uses: Wild celery was grown in medieval gardens because its seeds were thought to calm nerves, reduce gas and induce restful sleep. It was traditionally believed to be a stimulant.

Chervil, Sweet *(Myrrhis odorata)*
Other names: Sweet Cicely, Anise Fern
A tall, attractive perennial with fern-like leaves that smell strongly of anise.
Ancient uses: Infusion of sweet chervil root was thought to be an effective expectorant and a remedy for coughs. The large seeds were ground finely and used in 17th-century England for polishing floors and furniture.

Chive (*Allium schoenoprasum*)
Other name: Rush Onion
A dark-green perennial with hollow, cylindrical stems and lavender flowers.
Ancient uses: Chives are a very ancient herb; their use has been documented in China in 300 B.C. Once credited with stimulating appetite and suppressing a cough, chives are now used mostly for culinary purposes.

Cinnamon (*Cinnamomum zeylanicum*)
The aromatic bark of this evergreen is rolled into cylinders and dried.
Ancient uses: Cinnamon was once reputed to be a stimulant and an astringent. It is widely used as an aromatic and often added to spice teas as a "helper" flavor.

Coriander (*Coriandrum sativum*)
A very dainty annual with aromatic foliage and large, round whitish fruits.
Ancient uses: Coriander was traditionally believed to be a stimulant, restoring appetite and increasing vivaciousness. It was also credited with relieving headache and cardiac ailments.

Cumin (*Cuminum cyminum*)
A small, fragile herb with feathery foliage, cultivated chiefly for its seeds.
Ancient uses: A Greek proverb warns not to cut one's hand when splitting the cumin seed; misers were pejoratively called bean-splitters, and the cumin seed was too tiny even for the miser to split. Cumin was purported to aid cardiac ailments.

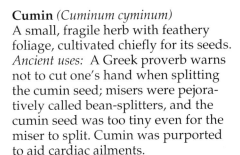

Dill (*Anethum graveolens*)
Other names: Dill Seed, Meetin' House Seeds
An elegant herb with blue-green, feathery leaves and tiny yellow flowers.
Ancient uses: Infusions of dill were reputed to eliminate hiccups and ease swelling and pain. Witches were said to hate it; a bunch of dill hung in the entryway was believed to rid the home of them.

Garlic (*Allium sativum*)
A tall plant with gray-green foliage and white flowers.
Ancient uses: In the Middle Ages, garlic was the poor man's panacea, believed to be the remedy for a host of afflictions including aches, pains, coughs, colds, asthma, bronchitis and pulmonary ailments.

Ginger (*Zingiber officinale*)
Other name: Jamaica Ginger
A tall plant with glossy leaves. The roots are dried and peeled, and the pungent, aromatic rhizomes are used.
Ancient uses: In the past, ginger tea was revered as a stimulant—to the palate as well as the rest of the body—and said to promote a feeling of warmth and well-being.

Horseradish (*Armoracia lapathifolia*)
A tall, pungent perennial with white flowers, grown primarily for its roots.
Ancient uses: Infusion of horseradish root was traditionally believed to induce perspiration and relieve toothache as well as facial neuralgia. Placed in the soles of shoes, the wilted leaves were thought to relieve weary feet.

Licorice (*Glycyrrhiza glabra*)
Other name: Sweet Wood
A leguminous perennial with paired pinnate leaves and blue flowers.
Ancient uses: Licorice-root tea was used to alleviate pulmonary ailments. The root was also employed to flavor cough medicines and it is still used in that capacity today.

Marjoram, Sweet (*Majorana hortensis*)
Commonly grown as a garden plant, this aromatic herb has attractive, dense flower clusters.
Ancient uses: The goddess Venus was said to favor marjoram. The tea was regarded as a potent stimulant and anti-inflammatory agent, and was reputed to chase incipient colds.

Mustard (*Brassica nigra—Black*)
(*Brassica alba—White*)
An annual herb with lobed leaves and bright yellow flowers.
Ancient uses: These ancient herbs were celebrated by Hippocrates and Pliny for their extensive medicinal value. Biblical references to mustards abound, usually comparing them in some way to man's faith.

Nutmeg (*Myristica fragrans*)
Other name: Mace
A tree with smooth, grayish-brown bark that produces an aromatic seed.
Ancient uses: Nutmeg has been traditionally credited with relieving nausea and alleviating cardiac ailments. Today its use is confined to culinary purposes.

Oregano (*Origanum vulgare*)
Other name: Wild Marjoram
A perennial with small leaves and purple or white flowers.
Ancient uses: The ancient Greeks valued oregano tea as a stimulant, and it was also believed to have great curative properties. Oregano was a symbol of happiness. Newly married couples were crowned with wreaths of it, and graves were planted with oregano beds with the hope that loved ones would rest in peace.

Parsley (*Petroselinum crispum*)
A strong biennial umbelliferous plant with tiny white or yellow flowers and aromatic leaves.
Ancient uses: Parsley was used by the Greeks to crown victorious Olympic athletes. When worn to a banquet, a parsley wreath absorbed alcohol fumes, thereby saving the wearer from drunkenness—or so the Romans believed.

Pepper, Black (*Piper nigrum*)
A woody vine with dark-green, aromatic leaves and red berries.
Ancient uses: Black pepper was once credited with stimulating appetite, probably lending to its great popularity as a condiment.

Peppermint (*Mintha piperita*)
Other name: Curled Mint
A dark-green, aromatic herb with lanceolate leaves and pink flowers.
Ancient uses: When taken as tea, peppermint was once reputed to be effective in alleviating stomach disorders. It was also revered for its cooling effect when added to throat preparations.

Poppy (*Papaver somniferum*)
Other name: Opium Poppy
A stout annual with gray-blue leaves and large red flowers.
Ancient uses: Although from the same plant used to produce opium, the poppy seeds used for culinary purposes do not have a narcotic effect. In ancient Greece, this common meadow plant was a love charm.

Raspberry (*Rubus idaeus*)
A canelike plant with small, round aggregate fruits.
Ancient uses: Raspberry was traditionally lauded as an effective astringent, used to clean wounds and ulcers. It was also used for mouthwash. Today raspberry is frequently infused to make a deliciously fragrant, caffeine-free tea.

Rose Hips (*Rosa canina*)
Other name: Wild Briar, Witches Briar
These are the ripened fruits of the wild rose.
Ancient uses: Well known to yield ascorbic acid (vitamin C), rose hips are popular infused to make a flavorful tea that has the added benefit of lacking caffeine. It has been said that American Indians did not suffer from scurvy because they so freely used rose hips.

Rosemary (*Rosmarinus officinalis*)
A small evergreen shrub with needle-like leaves and purple or blue flowers.
Ancient uses: Washing the skin with rosemary tea was believed to prevent aging. In England the herb was thought to bring good luck, break magic spells, cure insanity, headache and heartache.

Sage (*Salvia officinalis*)
Other name: Red Sage
A small perennial bearing bluish-purple flowers.
Ancient uses: Sage tea was traditionally believed to remedy stomach ailments and to induce perspiration, thereby combating colds and fever. If used by brunettes every week or so as a hair rinse, it was also thought to hide gray hair.

Savory, Summer (*Satureia hortensis*)
Other name: Bean Herb
A spindly annual with small leaves and lavender flowers.
Ancient uses: Infusion of summer savory was said to lighten a tanned complexion and alleviate colic. Fresh savory leaves pressed onto a bee sting were believed to relieve the pain.

Savory, Winter (*Satureia montana*)
A woody, dark-green perennial with small leaves and purple flowers.
Ancient uses: Traditionally lauded as an aid to childbirth, a stimulant and a potent aphrodisiac. Users were cautioned in *Bancke's Herbal* (1525) to use very sparingly in meat because "it stirreth him that useth to lechery."

Sesame (*Sesamum indicum*)
Other names: Semsem, Bene
A tall annual bearing white tubular flowers.
Ancient uses: Sesame is an ancient herb. Hippocrates lauded its numerous medicinal properties, and it was used to flavor wines over 6000 years ago.

Spearmint (*Mentha spicata*)
Other names: Our Lady's Mint, Sage of Bethlehem
A hardy, yellowish-green perennial.
Ancient uses: Spearmint was reputed to be a stimulant. President Theodore Roosevelt had a large bed of spearmint planted at the White House to enhance the beverages at meetings of his famous Tennis Cabinet.

Star Anise (*Illicium verum*)
Other names: Badian Anise, Chinese Anise
A small evergreen of the magnolia family cultivated for its star-shaped fruit.
Ancient uses: Star Anise was traditionally used as a stimulant and a diuretic. It was also believed to alleviate nausea.

Tarragon (*Artemisia dracunculus*)
Other name: French Tarragon
A bushy perennial with very narrow, pointed leaves and tiny yellow flowers.
Ancient uses: Reputed to be an effective diuretic, tarragon was also described as a specific for healing the bites of wild beasts and dogs. It was recommended by 13th-century botanists as a breath freshener.

Thyme (*Thymus vulgaris*)
Other name: Garden Thyme
An aromatic perennial with broad leaves and purple flowers.
Ancient uses: In medieval times, infusion of thyme was added to a tired soldier's bath to renew his vigor and braveness. It was also purported to be an antispasmodic and an antiseptic, especially for pulmonary ailments.

Turmeric (*Curcuma longa*)
A hardy perennial bearing deep-yellow, aromatic rhizomes.
Ancient uses: Turmeric was traditionally credited with rapidly relieving indigestion. Also, it was once highly regarded for its beneficial effects on the liver; however, it is not used medicinally very frequently today.

Vanilla (*Vanilla planifolia*)
A tropical, climbing orchid bearing yellow pods.
Ancient uses: Vanilla is often blended with other spices to make fragrant, full-bodied tea blends. Traditionally considered to be a stimulant, this herb was also believed to aid digestion and to act as an aphrodisiac.

Spice blends and herbal seasonings are treasured by gourmet cooks and culinary dabblers alike.

Those on limited diets will particularly appreciate the no-salt, no-caffeine blends. Tuck several packets of seasoning in a small basket with fruit and crackers.

In composing these flavorsome gifts, make sure your dried spices and herbs are not stale. Purchase new containers just before blending or use home-dried herbs from your garden. Almost any herb can be grown outdoors, and mint, rosemary, marjoram, basil, dill and tarragon do well in indoor containers, too. When grown indoors, parsley seems to be attractive to a certain variety of very small black fly, but as it is available at most supermarkets year-round, there is no excuse for not using it fresh.

If you have herbs in your own garden, it is not difficult to dry them yourself. To dry herbs, bundle them and hang them upside down in a warm, breezy place until they are bone dry; if not thoroughly dry, they can mold or rot. Check dryness by placing a few leaves in an airtight glass container for several days and watch for signs of mold, condensation or discoloration. If any of these signs occur, allow the herbs to dry longer.

All herbs should be stored in tightly closed jars or tins in a dry but not too hot place. Although a shelf above the stove is a common storage place for herbs and spices, they will lose their flavor rapidly when exposed to the high heat in this location.

Whether you use home-dried or store-bought, dried herbs should be crumbled before use to release flavor and aroma.

Mix herbs in china or glass bowls, as metal or plastic can impart an off taste. A tiny funnel folded of waxed paper will help you to fill jars and tins for giving. Seal each container tightly with tape around the edge of the lid to prevent herbs from dusting out in a package.

Although in this country herbs are used solely to enhance other foods, in many parts of the world they are served on their own as an appetizer. For alfresco summer dining, try a platter of freshly washed basil, mint, dill, parsley and coriander. Serve as is or with a bland cheese, scallions, cucumbers, radishes and tomatoes. Either way, you have a light and refreshing first course that will stimulate the palate for the good things to come.

seconds the iron is too hot.)

The transfer inks are printed in grey. Any instructions are printed in regular ink in another color. They are not intended to transfer but may, slightly, if the iron is hot.

For fabric: Wash fabric if it is heavily sized and iron out wrinkles. Place a sheet of clean white paper under fabric before ironing so the transfer ink will not pass through the layer of fabric onto whatever is beneath it. Set iron to correct heat for type of material. Avoid fabrics with more than 50% polyester.

1. Preheat your electric iron (don't use steam!). Cut out the the iron-on design with scissors so it contains only the areas you wish to transfer. Leave enough margin for pins or basting.

2. Use an ironing board with a firm surface. Position the design on your material, printed side down, so the ink is touching the material. If necessary, hold the paper in place with common pins or a basting stitch. The design may blur if the pattern moves while ironing.

3. Place and hold the iron on the back of the pattern paper for about 10 seconds wherever you want to transfer the printed design onto your material. Hold it longer for a darker image, a shorter time for a fainter one. If your iron has holes in the bottom they may break up the design. Reposition the iron slightly by lifting it and putting it down again. If you rub or wiggle the iron, the paper may shift slightly and blur the lines of the design.)

4. After about 10 seconds, remove the iron and peel back one small corner of the paper pattern to see if the ink has transferred to the fabric. If not, hold the iron in place 5 seconds longer and check again. (Approximately 25 seconds should always be enough.

Transfer Hints:

You may get as many as eight uses from your iron-on pattern.

Hold the iron in place about 5 seconds more after each reuse. After a few reuses, it may help to place a sheet of aluminum foil under the material to help conduct heat and transfer the ink. On fabric the ink will transfer better if you pass the hot iron over the material first to warm it before positioning the pattern and ironing it onto the material.

If you cannot see the transfer design (because the fabric is too dark, for example) trace it by hand. First iron it onto plain white paper. Place a sheet of carbon paper ("dressmaker" carbon for fabrics) between the white paper pattern and the material. Trace over the lines with a pen or pencil.

DOGWOOD MOTIF

STRAWBERRY MOTIF
Leaves, stems and tendrils: Green
Berries: Pink-to-red
Blossoms: edged in Pale Brown
Arrows indicate direction of shading
from light to dark

GRAPEVINE MOTIF
Leaves: Green
Vine and tendrils: Brown
Grapes: Blue
Arrows indicate direction of shading
from light to dark